STILL LIFE

with teapot

BRIGID LOWRY is the author of eight books for young adults, including best sellers *Guitar Highway Rose* and *Juicy Writing: Inspiration and Techniques for Young Writers.* She has an MA in Creative Writing and has taught writing at all levels, including at Curtin University. She spent seven years living in a Theravadin Buddhist community and is a long-time Zen student in the Diamond Sangha tradition. Her interests include social justice, creativity, travel, spirituality, and food. Her work explores what it is to be alive in the twenty-first century: this fertile, crazy, wonderful, scary moment in time.

book club notes and creative writing exercises available from fremantlepress.com.au

STILL LIFE with teapot

on zen, writing & creativity

BRIGID LOWRY

AMUSING THINGS

Things that look better from the back than the front

REGRETTABLE THINGS

THINGS THAT HAVE lost their power.

THINGS THAT ARE DISTANT THOUGH NEAR.

THINGS THAT MAKE THE HEART BEAT FASTER.

Endearingly lovely things

THE queen OF everything soup

The Queen of Everything Soup

I am The Queen of Everything Soup, but feel free to call me Madame Teapot, Moonbeam or Pencil Brain. I amuse myself by choosing a new creative name each day, inspired by the guy in Melbourne who changed his name to Very Impressive by deed poll in 1992. Go ahead, you can play too. How about Nasturtium, Shoe Dude, or Blue Happy?

Beyond my name, I am sixty-two years old, a woman living in a time and place moving so rapidly that I can't keep up. Have you heard the story about a man riding very fast on a horse? As he galloped past, his friend yelled, 'Where are you going?' 'I don't know, ask the horse,' the rider replied. I don't have a horse, but you get my meaning.

It's raining, and I'm making soup. This is my recipe.

Everything Soup. Choose your two oldest onions. Fry them gently with garlic, ginger, cumin, paprika, turmeric. Be lavish with spices. Chop whatever is in your crisper drawer: the shabby remnant of cabbage, half a withered capsicum, two carrots ... all vegetables are welcome here. Cover with water, add a tin of tomatoes, some frozen peas, a slosh of sweet chilli sauce, a blob of curry paste and a tablespoon of tomato paste if it hasn't gone mouldy.

Herbs are excellent: basil, parsley, spring onions, those last limp coriander leaves and stalks. Lemon zest, a can of chickpeas, leftover chicken if you're that way inclined. Bring to the boil and simmer gently. When the veggies are cooked add some miso. Dissolve it in a cup with some hot soup broth first so it doesn't remain a big lump. Serve in your favourite bowl, sprinkled with parmesan. It's divine with sourdough toast if you haven't given up an entire food group, such as dairy or carbs. My thought about this, by the way, is that unless you swell up and die when you eat something, there's no point avoiding it. Here's the thing: no matter how many gym visits or green smoothies you make, or vitamins you swallow, you won't escape old age, sickness and death, unless of course you die young. Meanwhile, why deny yourself cream on your pudding or yummy, oily pizza? Just saying. My views on this make me a tad unpopular with some of my friends and relatives, as you can imagine. Anyhow, what I was going to say, and forgive me for employing an obvious metaphor before we've got to know each other better, is that life is crazy abundant with all manner of things: haiku, petticoats, cancer, global warming, cucumbers, mountains, small children, slippers, turtles. There is Facebook and there are mice. It is Everything Soup, guys, and we are in it.

Fresh vibe, flower moon, strange path of life leading everywhere and nowhere ... Shirt sleeves, autumn melancholy, bright curtains, bouquets of hideous roses, a frayed green dress ...

What more do you need to know about me? Once I was almost beautiful, but now I have a wrinkly neck and sometimes go shopping with my cardigan inside out. I am twice divorced. No need to feel sorry for me. I don't regret my marriages and I'm nearly over the shock of my last husband suddenly preferring a dumpy woman from his fishing club. Mostly, I like being single. I have a lovely range of creative loungewear: floral pyjamas, vintage kimonos, soft dressing-gowns. I'm in complete command of the remote control. I do whatever I want whenever I want. Sometimes my dinner is last night's pad thai eaten in front of the telly. If I'm feeling particularly decadent I don't even heat it up. Ah, the wicked freedom of it! I was far too sensible when I was a wife.

I now have an invisible husband. When I change my mind about a supermarket purchase, I return it, explaining to the nice young chap at the service counter that my husband bought the wrong batteries, or got oat milk instead of almond milk. He gives me a refund, no worries, and we have a little chat about his latest hair colour. He seems to like me, although he must wonder why I have such a fuckwit of a husband.

I've decided to write a pillow book. I've always loved the famous one – *The Pillow Book of Sei Shōnagon*: a collection of observations written by a courtesan of Empress Consort Teishi in tenth-century Japan. I admire her lists, her elegant gossip, her fine eye for detail and dry sense of humour. I want to be her when I grow up, as well as Leunig, Leonard Cohen, Tom Waits, Jack Kerouac, Frida Kahlo, Sharon Creech, Helen Garner, Anne Lamott, Eloise, and Pippi Longstocking. I'd prefer not to have the deaths of Jack and Frida, just the creativity and colour. The good thing about being my age is that if you haven't grown up already, you don't have to. So I've decided to write a pillow book, because I have things to say about what it is to be an ageing woman living in the twenty-first century with as much dignity as she can manage, and saying these things out loud on the bus is probably not the best way to interface with the universe.

My book will be a good place for me to record my lists. Sei Shōnagon compiled lists on many topics: Surprising and distressing things; Amusing things; Things that look better from the back than the front. It's interesting how many of her observations are relevant today. For example, her list of Rare things includes a pair of silver tweezers that pull out hairs properly and a person who is without a single quirk.

I have always been in favour of lists. I make sensible ones: Buy pecan nuts, avocado. Post office. Bank. This serves the function of helping me feel that life is under control, even and especially when it isn't. The other kind of list is more fun. You pick a category and then record your observations, as Sei Shōnagon did.

> Annoying things: A sesame seed stuck in your teeth. Telephone numbers that are one digit short. Supergluing your fingers together. People who don't give a friendly wave when you make way for them in traffic.

> Wonderful things: Finding something is half-price when you were going to buy it anyway. Being the only one in your swimming lane. The spongy surface at kids' playgrounds. Scoring a purple leopard skin

jacket from a dress-up box. *New Yorker* cartoons. Mangoes. Stepping on a Cheezel and crunching it to smithereens.

Things one should not admit to: Preferring one's own company. Peeing in the sea. Peering into other people's medicine cupboards.

Interesting book titles: *5 Easy Steps to Becoming a Witch*; *Freud's Couch, Scott's Buttocks, Brontë's Grave*; *The Big Book of Lesbian Horse Stories*; *All My Friends Are Dead*; *Why Men Marry Bitches*; *The Pop-up Book of Phobias.*

Disagreeable things: Finding a hair in your food. Phone calls from strange call-centre people in India. Chain emails that ask you to send them on to eight amazing women who have changed your life.

Embarrassing old ladyish things: Starting a sentence then tapering off with 'Where was I going with that ...?' Bunions. Discovering, while in a cab on your way to the airport, an old bit of dental floss entwined in your necklace.

Okay, enough lists for now. I must get on with my day.

*

I live in a retirement complex. The residents are a motley crew. I haven't lived here long, but so far I've noted one of everything: one Asian lady, one blind woman, one raw-food cook, one gay guy, one definite alcoholic, one artist, one lady with Alzheimer's, one man with Parkinson's, one dude in a wheelchair. I am the one old hippy, which is why I am allowed to say 'dude'. I go downstairs, have a friendly, meaningless chat with the caretaker, and set off to visit my friend Marlena. We've started a club. It is called WUFWS (Wild Unpredictable Fools Who Sew). So far there are two of us. This is our mission statement:

> *We are constantly aware that we always have everything we need to fully enjoy the here and now. We try to get through each day with as much delight as possible. We pledge to include treats, fun, colour, creativity and silliness in our lives on a daily basis.*

It's the best club I've ever been in. It's only the second one, actually. When I was eight I went to Girl Guides, once. We were given a jolly activity: to see who could write their name fastest using crumbled-up Weetabix. I decided I'd rather be at home reading a book. I've never been much of a joiner, but I like being a wild unpredictable fool who sews.

Marlena lives in a terrace house not far from my place. She's extraordinarily untidy. I remind her I'm not the housework police but as always she apologises profusely, sweeping a mound of clean, unfolded laundry off her sofa so I can sit down. She brews a pot of lapsang souchong and scrabbles around until she finds some biscotti. We haul out our sewing and begin. Marlena is appliquéing vintage roses onto a calico bag. I'm darning a maroon merino jumper.

Mending things is my way of honouring the worn and the shabby. I don't want people in sweatshops in Bangladesh making me new stuff. There is too much stuff in this world and not enough savouring of what we already have, in my opinion.

One of the things I love about my friend is that she talks all the time so I don't need to. I listen, contributing an affirmative word here and there, while Marlena's intelligent mind ranges far and wide and back again.

'Was reading my horoscope yesterday in a magazine. It promised all sorts of good things, including clarity in my financial doings and a possible love interest in June. It really resonated, until I realised I'd been reading Taurus.'

We hoot with laughter, because she's a Pisces. Unlike me, Marlena wants a love interest. She's been lonely since her husband died four years ago and wishes for some companionship in this crazy thing called life. As for me, since my marriage ended, I have had several minor odd encounters with the male species, as follows:

One: I was waiting in a long queue at a government office one Tuesday morning when a Romanian man started talking to me. He was short but not unattractive, and he was a very smooth talker.

'Beautiful woman, your brown eyes entrance me. I want to take you special places. You deserve happiness, you are a flower of loveliness.' I could have snubbed him, but the queue was lengthy and oh, what the hell. We talked about gypsy music, the weather and Middle Eastern food. 'May I telephone you? I will take you out for a lovely dinner. I will treat you like a princess.' Feeling idiotic, I gave him my phone number. He called that evening, drunk, begging me to come to his flat so he could feel my bosoms. 'Inappropriate,' I said and hung up. Thankfully he did not call back.

Two: At Marlena's insistence, I had one attempt at internet dating. The man sounded interesting enough: a photographer who liked to travel. Sadly, he turned out to be a lonely stoner who reeked of stale smoke. When I said I wasn't interested in having a relationship, playing the I'm Not Over My Marriage card, he asked very straightforwardly, 'Fair enough, how about sex then?' I wasn't sure if he meant right then or just in general but I explained that, for me, sex was not a treat like ice-cream you had on the side but a joyous part of a committed relationship, then gently turfed him into the night. Next morning he messaged me with, 'I should be waking up with you in my arms instead of sitting here staring at this bloody piece of toast,' which was endearing, but not endearing enough to make me change my mind. I will stick with my tiny crush on the man at the post office, who is ten years younger than me and possibly gay, but who has a kind face and wears colourful shirts. When I buy stamps, we talk. I pretend we're flirting, but no doubt he just finds me odd. I remain content to live alone, except for the moth residing in my kitchen who flies out from behind electrical appliances now and again.

However, Marlena has not given up her quest for a significant other, despite having met a whole lot of nothing so far. Her latest coffee date was with a spindly man in his seventies whose hobby was frequenting the airport at odd hours in order to photograph minor sports stars arriving or departing. He'd arrived at their meeting place, a garden cafe, clutching two hefty albums of these gems to show her.

'I told him I didn't believe in sports, and got the hell out of there. Perhaps I should become a lesbian?' she says, offering me the biscuit tin again. I grin in an accepting manner, indicating I'm broad-minded, if you'll pardon my pun, and take another biscotti.

'The thing is,' she continues, 'I really like cock.' This makes me laugh so hard I splutter tea and crumbs everywhere. Marlena loves to shock people. 'I had my best sex with my third husband in hotels because you could get oil all over the sheets and not worry about it,' she'll say gaily, or 'I was in a hot tub after a retreat in California with a Zen rōshi and I saw his wrinkled little scrotum.' She does it to amuse herself at book club when things get tedious.

Young people think we are just boring old people. They are wrong. There are things I haven't told you yet.

*

Once I was mad and lived on the edge of nowhere, planting silver beet and bright nasturtiums, slowly gardening the days away and folding myself into the corners of the night, folding time into squares of old newspaper and cutting the squares into stars and hearts and rows of paper dolls. I slept by myself under a blue quilt and ate bread and cheese dipped in soup from a Chinese bowl. I loved a man who didn't love me. It was an old story and a sad story and nobody cared a fig.

Or maybe they did. Certainly everyone in my house had advice for me.

Keep busy, Bella, said my grandmother, you must keep

busy. Crisp syllables slipped from her lips like dried leaves or scraps of old paper and as she spoke her brown fingers knew no rest, deftly chopping oranges into slices for marmalade. Keep busy, she said. It has always worked for me. She slid the oranges into a white bowl and left them there to soak and soften. My grandmother put on her sunflower earrings and off she went, looking as cheerful as the sun itself, off down the street to play bridge.

How can he have done this to you? asked my sister. For you are so beautiful, said my sister, as if lust or happiness or loneliness were influenced by beauty. You can borrow my lipstick, my sister said, my good necklace, my white shirt, anything you fancy as long as you don't get it dirty, and then she fossicked around for her car keys and vanished for days on end. In country towns on slow afternoons, librarians bought textbooks from my sister and at night she ate steak and chips in the motel restaurant, and dreamed of sticky date pudding and a large bank balance and a new pair of shoes.

Plenty more fish in the sea, said my father, a sensible man of few words. He was not concentrating properly, having one eye and the best part of his mind on the evening weather report. Ants in my pants. Bats in my belfry. Fish in the sea. Perhaps he was right. Down to the shoreline I went, searching for mermaids and filling my pocket with tiny, purple shells. I asked the time of a rather nice seahorse. I knew in my heart that not just any old fish would do.

And still my life stretched out ahead like a curse or a blessing.

You must eat properly, said my mother. The worst thing you can do is not eat. She fed me porridge with walnuts and honey, fish cakes with herbs, nectarines and cream. My cheeks grew pink and my thighs grew plump but still my nights were lonely and the sheets on my bed were cold to my exploring touch.

My grandfather said nothing, but he sat with me on the veranda until mosquitoes and stars came dancing out. I rolled his cigarettes for him from a tin of dark tobacco, fragrant shreds poking out of the neat, white twists. He played a tango for me on his piano accordion, the tattoos of all the women he had loved and lost fading on his wrinkled, hairy arms. My mother brought us sticky semolina cake drenched in orange juice. Ever so quietly my heart began to mend.

Then wouldn't you just know it? Out of the blue, who should ring but the unreliable man himself. How are you, he asked, my faithless lover, leaving no gap for my reply. Things have changed, he told me, his voice as slippery as a wet lizard. I need to talk to you, he wheedled, and begged me to go to dinner at our old familiar place.

Not with you, I told him, not tonight, not tomorrow, not ever, not ever again. I am too busy, I told him, and these are some of the many things that are far more interesting than you. I have much advice to listen to, a garden to weed, plump thighs to squeeze into old blue jeans, and a pocket full of shells to arrange on my window ledge and anyway, I told him, I have met somebody else. Actually, I intend to get married, I said, to a seahorse, sometime around the end of next week. And I did, carrying a bouquet of red nasturtiums and surrounded by my bridesmaids, a merry row of dancing paper dolls.

Okay, that wasn't exactly true, but it nearly was. Our lives are not solid. They are stories that twist over time. Cobwebs, smoke, mirrors. Fictional accounts, not facts.

*

I like facts. I collect unusual ones, as follows: A Bird Poop Facial at the Shikuza New York Day Spa costs $180, promises to brighten and nourish the complexion, and involves sitting for an hour with a mask of rice bran, water and powdered nightingale droppings on your face. During one of his periods of insanity, King George III insisted on ending every sentence he spoke with the word 'peacock'. Ancient Swedes practised euthanasia by leaving their elders to die after putting them into earthenware jars. Bill Gates paid $34.6 million for Leonardo Da Vinci's notebook. According to Native American Indian myth, a dog with two different coloured eyes can see both heaven and earth.

Apart from facts, I collect teacups, old postcards, neurotic friends, recipes, scarves and decent pens. What else can I tell you? There are days on which I talk out loud to bumblebees, days on which all my yesterdays rise up to meet me in the taste of lemon verbena tea, or the smell of clean washing. I have never drunk a cup of coffee or a glass of beer, but when I was a kid I owned two goldfish named Tweedledum and Tweedledee. I recently bought a book titled *How To Write a Damn Good Novel*, for a dollar, in an op shop. Once upon a time I fell in love with a beautiful young man in a park in New York. He never knew. We were both watching an exceptionally good band in Washington Square Park. New York is my most beloved city. I'd like to go there one more time. I'll stop off in Hawaii, put a red hibiscus behind my ear, enjoy some pedal steel guitar. I travel frequently, in my imagination; a wonderful place without airport queues, sneezing people or tropical diseases.

Disappointing things: Missing the train. Some haircuts. A phone that stops ringing just as you pick it up. Dry, tasteless mandarins.

Things I've overheard in cafes: 'I'm tired of falling over and bumping and bruising myself.' 'He's not stalkerish or anything, just keen.' 'Getting married before you are thirty is like leaving a party before 10pm.' 'Compared to an electron, a flea's balls are really big.'

Dreams you're glad to wake up from: Dream in which you are unsuccessfully trying to organise hundreds of small children into a circle to play a word game. Dream in which you look strange because you have lost several front teeth. Long convoluted dream involving expensive hair products and being locked in a cupboard.

Sei Shōnagon's lists: Things that have a hot feel. Things that have lost their power. Things that are distant though near. Things that make the heart beat faster. Things that arouse a fond memory of the past. Things without merit. Things that fall from the sky.

Regarding the last: Rain. Sleet. Snow. Meteorite fragments. A leaf. A feather. A wish. A prayer. Can't think of anything else ...

I wander around the room, not sure where to go next, so I google 'Things that fall from the sky'. Apparently frogs, worms, non-dairy creamer, a cow, golf balls, meat, a human body, money, blood, a rain of spiders, star jelly fish (whatever they are), multicoloured snow, and hundreds of starlings have fallen from the sky, though not all at the same time. Who knew? Still not sure where to go next, I eat a piece of cake, paint my toenails and don't write another word for three weeks.

Later, much later. Ate a button. I know! How, you may well ask, or indeed, why?

I was on the patio removing tight elastic from my pyjama pants and drinking green tea. Once I'd have dealt with a few extra kilos by living on cottage cheese and rice crackers but contentment is my current aim. No one but me minds my lumpy bits. I don't imagine the moth has an opinion about it.

First I unpicked three small black buttons, serving no purpose other than decorative, and put them down beside me on the coffee table. It was lovely, sitting dreamily in the idle afternoon warmth. Then I picked up a little black button, popped it in my mouth and washed it down with a swig of tea. It was a reflexive action, the one I do each morning when I take a multivitamin with my morning cuppa. No real harm done. It will make its innocent way through my body, no doubt. I don't know whether this counts as a strange thing I did by mistake, because technically I did it on purpose.

*

Not much has happened lately. For now, I've lost Marlena. She's gone to Bali with an almost handsome man she met on the train. She's left town with no return address. She died in her sleep. She's a character I invented that I'm considering abandoning. I'm not even sure I want to write a book any more. All I seem to have is many lists and facts and not enough narrative. Once upon a time the peonies were in full bloom and there were no cell phones or traffic cops and everyone was fairly cheerful, except when they weren't. This is the true story of my life. Except it isn't.

I wonder what it would be like to eat a cherry blossom? I also wonder if there's a word for the misreading of things, such as thinking it says 'Driver Under Reconstruction' on the front of a bus when it actually says 'Driver Under Instruction', or reading a headline as 'Deadly Tomato Hits America' instead of 'Deadly Tornado'? Today I read 'The room had its own silliness' instead of 'The room had its own stillness.'

> Sign of wandering loneliness: Almost telling the very bored girl in the posh underwear store that my son and his wife have bought a small dog.

Life goes on. It's autumn. I feel the usual melancholy. Despite despising capitalism, I go shopping and buy a duvet, white and soft as a cloud, and a decent wooden chopping board, although I perversely continue to use my stained old plastic one because I don't want to spoil the new one. Life is full of paradox. For example, you can be glad you are no longer married to someone but miss them unbearably at times. Our days were good and now they're gone. Where are you now? Are you happy? When will I grow up enough to stop referring to your new wife as Slutty Pants?

Maybe I will never kiss anyone again. I dream of making love with M, her small unsatisfactory breasts. I remember old boyfriends, my own foolishness, theirs, long summers, beaches, the awful brown linen dress my mother made me, the exact moment I was told my father had killed himself. In the park today children were playing in the branches of a tree, a noisy flock of wingless creatures, hidden by leaves. One called out in glee, 'Now we are in an upside down world!' I felt joyous and incredibly alone.

Did you know that you can use the inside of a banana skin to polish leather boots and shoes. I wonder who discovered this? Did they also try rubbing kiwi fruit on bloodstains, oranges on ink stains, strawberries on warts? Here's to them, whoever they were, spending happy mad hours doing weird stuff with fruit.

Furthermore, as G. K. Chesterton says, 'The poets have been mysteriously silent on the subject of cheese.' And who can blame them ...

*

Scary times! I go to buy an egg beater and they don't exist anymore. Not in fancy kitchen shops, anyhow. 'Do you mean a whisk?' the saleswoman asks. 'No,' I say, 'an egg beater.' I follow her to a wall of hanging kitchen gadgets, including a vast range of whisks. 'I want an egg beater,' I tell her, and begin to mime using one in a slightly desperate manner. 'Oh, I remember,' she says. 'I think my mother had one of those.' She looks about forty. I feel like an ancient crone who's asked for a butter churner, and speak gaily about my Bamix, to prove I am not completely last century. Then I go to buy some breadcrumbs and read on the label: Breadcrumbs, Cereal and Cereal Flours, Wheat, Thiamine Foliate, Rye, Barley, Water, Yeast, Iodised Salt, Soy Flour, Gluten, Vegetable Oil (Canola), Vegetable Fibre (Wheat, Soy6), Vinegar, Sugar, Emulsifiers, (Vegetable) (471, 481, 472e0).

I wander home feeling dispirited. Breadcrumbs used to be just crumbed bread without a number in sight, and everybody had an egg beater. I eat two pieces of toast with ricotta and marmalade to cheer myself up, which is exactly what old ladies do, I realise, live on toast and jam. Oh Lord, it's all downhill now. Yet I consider it my holy duty not to go completely sad and mental about ageing. As Voltaire said, 'The best thing you can do for this world is be in a good mood.' Famous men of long ago offered much wise and pithy advice, although Proust seems a man of contradiction. He suggested you should 'always try to keep a piece of sky above your life' but also wrote that he was 'dispirited after a dreary day with the prospect of a depressing morrow.' I prefer the note left by the boy king, Ludwig II of Bavaria, for his servant saying 'Remind me to look happier tomorrow.'

The obsolescence of egg beaters and the impurity of breadcrumbs has left me feeling squirrelly. Squirrelly is a real word, meaning restless, jumpy, nervy. I make a cup of tea and read the newspaper my neighbour has left for me. She's ninety-two and sharp as a tack, a dignified woman with so many things wrong with her body that her world has shrunk to the size of her apartment and her only outing is using her walker to take her rubbish down to the bin, very slowly.

In the paper I read about priests, forbidden to sleep with women, who fiddle around with young boys instead. Metals giant Nyrstar will continue to emit dangerous levels of lead pollution at their Port Pirie smelter until 2017, despite the fact that twenty-five percent of children in the area have dangerous levels of lead in their blood. A woman lost her arm in a mincer. Reading the paper is not helping my mood. I shall cheer myself up with some lists and perhaps a fact or two.

> Things that bring a strange delight: Finding one's wallet after thinking one has lost it. A young man carrying a bunch of flowers. Arriving at the station to find your train is due in one minute. People who thank the bus driver as they disembark. Little girls in fairy dresses.

> Interesting book titles: *God: The Interview*; *Knitting with Dog Hair*; *Creamy and Crunchy: An Informal History of Peanut Butter*; *Goblinproofing One's*

Chicken Coop; Still Life with Psychotic Squirrel; I am a Strange Loop.

Handy acronyms: PEBCAK – Problem exists between chair and keyboard. WIOYM – Wish I'd ordered your meal. PDDNOS – Pervasive developmental disorder not otherwise specified – an educational term describing what used to be called 'a bit thick'. FUBAR – Fucked up beyond all recognition. CFI – Complete fucking idiot.

Not sure when I can use any of these but glad I have them in my repertoire.

Things I don't understand: Who thinks up jokes. Why container ships don't sink. Why some days I love my life and other days I'm bewildered by it. How to play chess. People who text while riding a bicycle.

Great lines I wish I'd written: I wasn't happy but my hair looked good. When my mother was in the mood, we were Catholic. At Christmas we ate beetroot out of a tin; it tasted of disappointment. When ten people tell you you're drunk, sit down. Wednesdays are a very busy month for me.

In the tenth century, Abdul Kassem Ismael, grand vizier of Persia, couldn't bear to part with his 117,000-volume library. When he travelled, his books were carried by a caravan of four hundred camels, trained to walk in a way that preserved the library's alphabetical order.

Ink, by volume, is twice as expensive as French perfume. While we are on things vaguely related to literature, do you realise that every book, poem, play or song you've ever read is just a combination of twenty-six letters? The more you think about this, the more miraculous it becomes.

*

Did I mention that quite some time has passed without a word written? I wonder if Sei Shōnagon's writing sometimes deserted her? Was the muse her constant companion or did she spend hours gazing out her window, hoping a line of poetry might appear? I see her there, wearing a green kimono, shiny black hair caught up in an ivory clasp, but I don't know the answer to my question. As for me, my kimono is blue satin with chrysanthemums and the days drift by.

However, several things have happened of late. Firstly, Marlena has met a man. His name is Harvey, which in itself is not promising. He's not bad looking for an older man but I don't like him. He cut his sandwich into pieces and ate it with a knife and fork. He took more than his share of salad, didn't help clear the table, and did a fair bit of name-dropping. Rilke wrote: 'I want to be with those who know secret things or else alone.' Harvey doesn't seem to be the sort of man who knows secret things. He seems more like 'all hat and no cattle', as they say. I want to tell her not to hook up with this douchebag, but she already has. They're planning a weekend away in Margaret River, and are talking about travelling together in Europe next winter. Not my circus, not my monkeys, as the Polish proverb goes but I'm not good at staying out of other people's business. This morning, while preparing my breakfast, I was wondering whether to offer my nephew some advice. Lost in contemplation, I forgot to pay attention to the slice of walnut bread I'd popped down for further toasting, thus burning it to buggery and answering my question at the same time. Forget about fixing others, and focus on my own life. Another incredible insight and all before the day's first cup of tea.

Anyhow, strange times. Having decided to embrace being single, I met a guy at a book launch. I was seduced by his interesting texts and the fact that he knew a thing or two about Jung. Three weeks of intensity followed. I pashed him on my bed. A mistake. Not only was his kiss like thrusty tongue rape, he turned out to be, as Milton so elegantly put it, deep versed in books and shallow in himself. Almost immediately another man turned up at my door, a skinny, charming songwriter with whom I must not fall in love, due to the fact that he is married. In a weird trilogy, a third gentleman arrived on the edges of my life. This one wore nice hats and had a shitload of money, but also a wife and a longstanding mistress. It seems all the men I meet are crazy makers. I decide to be in love with myself and dance alone in my lounge at midnight wearing a silk nightgown, feeling vaguely foolish.

I must remember to align my behaviours with my core values: Live simply. Seek the joyous.

Perhaps it's not too late to have a happy childhood. Today

I drew with coloured pencils, and saw a picture book in the library titled *Boom, Snot, Twitty*, which cheered me up tremendously. This world does not have enough silly in it for my liking. I read somewhere that everyone needs ten percent nonsense in their life. When I mentioned this to Marlena she suggested, 'Let's make that ninety percent.'

Another lovely thing was overhearing a small boy say to his mother in the supermarket, 'Let's buy some stuff and make a bit of a party tonight.' Apart from that, it was one of those days when everyone looked a bit odd, including the little fat lady with her matching little fat dog, and a bizarre man of about eighty, dressed in a scanty lycra sports outfit, his skin as wrinkled as an elephant's.

Now I'm home and I've done all my chores. What next? I could google how to deliver a baby in a taxi or how to fold a fitted sheet or how to dance the Argentinian tango. Or I could just sit quietly, looking out my window at the sunset, soft icy pink fading to grey, listening to the farewell songs of birds, letting the night-time fall.

The more powerful and original a mind, the more it will incline towards the religion of solitude. Aldous Huxley said this. Very encouraging. I feel much better about living alone, in quiet companionship with the moth.

A confession. Three times in my life I've thrown a beverage at someone. I can't even remember why, in my forties, standing on her veranda, I threw a teacup at my best friend or what compelled me, when we shared a flat in our twenties, to pour cocoa over my cousin's hair just as she was leaving for work. It's odd what you remember, or forget. It's all in there somewhere, apparently, hidden in our neural pathways: every book read, every flower picked, every mistake made, every tomato tasted. But accessing it gets tricky. We accept that eyesight fails, that knees and hips need replacing, and that hearing declines, but we're so terrified of dementia that we resist admitting the frailty of memory. Yesterday I began telling Marlena I'd had my foot x-rayed but my brain came up with 'I've had my foot emailed.' Hearing loss can be amusing, too. This morning I had an interesting conversation with my neighbour in which I thought we were discussing wheat packs but she turned out to be talking about Weetbix. Later, my crusty Yorkshire man neighbour gave me some bus timetables. It was kind of him. I thanked him profusely and gave him a hug. Note to self: In future, don't. It seemed to terrify him. He's an interesting guy though. Now in his eighties, he wears shorts every day of the year except very occasionally when he dresses more formally and goes to the opera. His description of Easter: More people on the streets and fewer buses. He used to be a cartographer who worked in Midland. Once a year he goes there on the train and says out loud, 'I'm glad I don't work here any more.' Then he gets on the train and comes home.

Things that might happen tomorrow: I might see a famous person. I might die of a heart attack. I might see a rainbow over the ocean.

An idea I read in a magazine: Write at least one good thing that happens each day and put it in a jar, so that at the end of the year you have 365 good things that have happened to you, on pieces of paper, in a jar.

Lately my dreams have been very vivid. In the strange movie of sleep, my old clothes don't fit me anymore and my sisters walk away, leaving me in an amphitheatre of nasturtiums. In real life I bought some new trousers. Black, with black satin trim around the pockets, and quite flattering. My former best trousers have become my second best trousers. What else? Marlena has cooled towards Harvey because he makes racist comments. She was so hopeful about him but, as she's a dedicated old leftie, this is a deal-breaker. Secretly I'm glad. I want my friend to be happy but she deserves better.

'Maybe you and I can go down south,' I offer. 'We could have picnics and walk by the sea.'

'That would be nice,' she replies, but wistfully. We both know it probably won't happen. We sit and sew together, and eat some of the date loaf I'd made. For once my friend does not talk like mad.

*

I'm getting a sense about the people living in my retirement complex: the relentlessly cheerful woman, the frail man who stutters yet tries to flirt a little, the folk who are prone to laundry wars. This is my home now, and these are my people. I wonder what they make of me, going down to the rubbish bins at odd hours wearing my kimono, turning off my lights at midnight, not surfacing until late in the day? What I like best about people is how flawed we all are, and how magnificent. My yoga teacher has smelly armpits. My Zen teacher could lose a little weight. All of us just ordinary people, doing the best we can.

Lately, quietly, I've been discarding possessions: my turmeric-stained floral apron, the worn-out red shoes of my old life. I feel lighter. I've been doing a lot of thinking, about all manner of things. About letting go and living in the moment, which I appreciate intellectually but mainly do not do. I've been drinking my tea slower, and remembering that, in a far-off land, someone picked these tea leaves for me.

I've also been contemplating the lack of festivities and ceremonies in our culture. Thai people celebrate Songkran, giving their homes a thorough spring-cleaning, discarding broken things lest they bring bad luck to the owner. The Balinese calendar has auspicious days for rice planting, starting a business, digging wells, making laws, castrating animals, cutting hair and learning to dance. They've a specific deity for artists and writers, Saraswati, who rides a white swan and has four arms, each holding creative gifts. The Balinese are on to it, for sure. My favourite Balinese celebration is Tumpek Landep, a day devoted to the God of Metal, when blessing ceremonies are performed for weapons, cars and metal tools, giving them magical powers and efficiency. It's also considered a time for sharpening the mind. Our culture is lacking. We only have weddings and funerals. I think we should have auspicious days for baking cakes and getting divorced, and festivals to celebrate new babies and mountains and teapots.

In my local paper a kid called Milo Sprod was mentioned,

which led me to thinking about names. I admire people who name their children Poet and Arlo, but not those who call their children T'lah or Jaxxon. I don't think you should call your child Kahlua, Diammond-Sparckle, Hippo, Burger or Google, all of which were officially registered names in Australia in 2012. Furthermore, spell names correctly, please. Don't go with Ameigh or Fynn.

Yesterday a young Korean Mormon knocked on my door. He tried to give me a little card but I shook my head, said, 'No thank you,' and gently shut the door before he had a chance to speak. After he'd gone, I realised I could have said, 'I'm busy, darling, researching German pornography, but you're welcome to come in and discuss theology with my moth.' Obviously I am not the steadiest peanut in the pack but this thought amused me for some time.

*

I wake this morning feeling low. No avoiding the miseries, sometimes. As Janet Frame wrote: 'Dead, over, gone. How we accept it, in flowers.' My mood is not helped by reading a review of play in which a woman tried to dissuade her husband from leaving her by climbing on top of him, and pleading. Maybe I should have tried that, I say to the moth, who as usual, makes no comment. Which is why I love the moth.

However, I still feel crap. I want to run away to New Mexico and open a cafe. I want to say to someone dreary 'Let's not have coffee.' I want to buy an art piece I read about, a collage of old horoscopes and unpicked clothes labels, entitled *And None of It Was Me*. I want windows of moonlight and sea breezes, a pen that writes in Spanish. I want to float down a river on a lotus blossom, letting the moonlight guide me. Instead, I take the train to town, to Kakulas Brothers, and buy cashew nuts and spices. I need to get out of my apartment, to be amongst people, amongst life. I wander around in the sunshine in the city, making up new names for people: The Jesus girl, Silly Trousers, Edna-the-Phone-Queen. I observe young men with odd modern beards, drink a rose-water lassi at Govinda's, listen to a busker playing 'Brown Eyed Girl' at the train station. By the time I get home I'm happy again.

Peaceful things: A sleeping cat. The day after the day after Christmas. A garden.

Poignant things: A child's sock or shoe, abandoned in a park. A late night bus carrying no one but the driver.

Amusing things: A teenage boy's dreadlock, used as a bookmark. Jamie's Fifteen Minute Meal of rice, okra and chicken that took my friend all day to make.

Things I like that other people probably don't like: Slightly rancid butter. Getting the daily paper, late in the day, from the rubbish bin outside my local cafe.

Things I don't like that other people like: Reality TV. Botox. Alcohol. Coffee. iPods. Twitter. Conclusion: I have been born in wrong century.

More conclusions: Golf is marbles for grownups. Macaroons are biscuits for people with too much money.

*

I don't know where the days go but now it's early October and Christmas cards and baubles are appearing in the shops. Too soon, she cried! While we are on the subject of silly madness, a swanky restaurant is serving a dish of crisp-skinned pork belly pieces with chewy, salty pig's ear strands, garnished with scorched ants. Seriously! Oh, foolish rich people! I savour my avocado on toast, feeling superior.

A new day. I do my laundry and vacuum, glad I live in a country not ripped apart by war or famine. I need to hang a picture on my wall but it takes some time to work out how to tell the handyman I want a screw, without sounding as though I'm asking him for a shag. I take a jar of marmalade to my neighbour, who comes out with some very wise things despite the fact that he drinks red wine for breakfast. We discuss life, the universe and everything and he sums it up with 'Shit happens and life goes on.' Even the Buddha could not have put it better.

Things I wonder: When did chemists start selling homewares? When did Post Offices start selling all sorts of weird shit? Did anyone ever actually say Totes Amazeballs or did it go straight to irony?

Things you should have learned by the time you are sixty: Always check the toilet seat before you sit down in a public toilet. If you stop trying to please people, your life will be both easier and happier. The earlier you think you are, the later you will become. It is helpful to know someone with a lemon tree. There is no housework police. Comfort trumps style, but aim for both. There is no other moment.

Mantra for use when walking through Ikea: *I don't need any more pillows. I don't need any more candles.*

Seven habits of highly annoying people: Asking how you are, not listening to your reply, and ten minutes later asking how you are. Making half a plan then failing to confirm. Tooting at you immediately the lights change. Saying 'We must have coffee' but not meaning it. Describing their disastrous life on their phone, incredibly loudly, on the train. Saying coochie-coo stuff to their dog in the middle of you telling them something really important. Telling you about someone else's fabulous cooking in the middle of eating the meal you cooked for them.

In case you are wondering, the third time I threw a beverage, it was orange juice, over my young son, in a food hall, when he hassled me one too many times for more coins to lose in the video machine. You will be glad to learn that he's turned out exceptionally well, despite this dreadful behaviour by his mother.

Marlena and I decide the Wild Unpredictable Fools Who Sew need a new activity. We choose yarn bombing.

Sourcing the wool is fun; it involves searching in cupboards, op-shopping, and dismantling old knitwear. We find yarns and braids and ribbons in every colour: red, green, pale and dark blue, pink, crimson, orange, purple, yellow, turquoise, black, white. When the sun goes down we venture to the park and wrap up a bench. It takes ages but it turns out magnificently, all woolly rainbows and bobbles. Total class.

*

Spring. A time of blue trees. Jacaranda blossoms above and beneath. On Halloween, children take to the streets, parents draggling behind, in search of lollies. I take to the streets to admire them: little wizards and witches, bandaged boys and tiny ghostie girls, older elegant witches, a tall boy with fake blood dripping from his mouth, Kermit arm-in-arm with Superman, those without real costumes but only a pirate eye patch – and my favourite, the lad with a green chequered box on his head.

It feels odd, wandering the streets, watching them, like some kind of ancient vampire who feasts on the sight of the young, but one of the blessings of age is a kind of invisibility. They are so excited by the chocolate and sweeties they're stashing in their plastic pumpkins they don't even notice me. I might be a tree or a cloud.

These days I try not to worry so much about being normal because who amongst us is normal? There's just you and me and the man talking to himself on the crazy seat and the guy with the sign saying *Hopeless* begging outside the railway station and the posh woman wearing too much make-up and the fat kid and the beautiful thirteen-year-old in her floral dress and six old ladies playing cards at the bowling club. We're all one pen short of a stationery cupboard, one way or another.

As for wishing to be younger, well, not that either. When we were younger we shaved we tweaked we blushed we fluffed but sometimes we couldn't be bothered. We listened to the radio late at night and wondered if anyone would ever love us, we listened to the kinks the beatles the stones the animals the who. We worried about our hair we worried about our weight we were too thin too fat we wanted a man with a good sense of humour who did not laugh at our bad perm we wanted a baby we didn't want a baby we thought we might never find a man who wanted to give us a baby we loved the smell of our dear wee milky baby we put cucumber slices and teabags on our eyes we put our elbows in half lemons to make them whiter we sellotaped our fringe to our forehead and cut our own wonky fringes we used veet which smelled foul we shaved our legs but it made the hairs more bristly sometimes we nicked our ankles and they bled we let our legs get hairy we wanted to be beautiful some of us were already beautiful but we didn't know it some of us were plain ...

These are my thoughts on a bee-hum spring day, a cheerful day, on which I want to say yen and oft for no particular reason.

While roasting vegetables for lunch I listen to a radio program about seahorses, which did you know are actually fish? Seahorse courtship lasts for several days, during which time they may change colour. They swim side by side holding tails or grip the same strand of sea grass with their tails, then wheel around in unison before the female impregnates the male. Throughout the gestation period of several weeks, the female visits the male daily for morning greetings. They interact for about six minutes, reminiscent of courtship. The female then swims away until the next morning, and the male returns to sucking up food through his snout, all of which has a certain elegant charm, n'est-ce pas?

*

Marlena called to say she's definitely parted ways with Harvey. Whoo hoo, I think, but give a more measured response. 'Want to come over tomorrow? We could yarn bomb my old bicycle?' Marlena agrees, and says she'll bring orange almond cake, my favourite. Women do many things when their hearts are aching. Baking is one of them.

More odd book titles: *The Long Dark Tea-time of the Soul. Tea Bag Folding. The Hollow Chocolate Bunnies of the Apocalypse. How to Be an Adult. To Save Everything, Click Here. Tobacco and Your Mouth: The Incredibly Disgusting Story.*

Real words you probably won't get to use very often: Honeyfuggle: to deceive or swindle, by flattery. Bumfuzzle: to confuse. Quisling: A traitor, especially one who aids an invading enemy. Furfuraceous: covered with dandruff.

Good words I have invented: Flumped, as in, she flumped on her bed. Not-sureification. Pretendy-getz. Happarillo. A bit of a fruck-off. Wunky: wonderful in a way that is not at all clunky. Duhthang: thing bought when you are tired which you later regret buying. Igblob: extra bit you throw in when cooking rice or pasta that ends up being too much. Schlumpy: food eaten while standing at bench.

Comforting things: Polar fleece. Rose-scented soap. Hot lemon, ginger and honey.

Sei Shōnagon's lists: People who seem to suffer. Enviable people. Things that gain by being painted. Things that lose by being painted. Things that cannot be compared. Things without merit.

Things I should get rid of: My daggy bathing suit. Friends who whinge a lot. My old plastic chopping board, so I can't possibly use it.

Currently my holy task is smiling practice. I've stuck a card on my bathroom mirror which says, 'If you're happy, tell your face.' I'm also practising ōryōki, a Japanese practice meaning Just Enough. It's profound, this gentle practice of enoughness. Enough food on my plate, enough clothes in my wardrobe, accepting whatever comes my way. Not demanding that life give me more or different. As the wise ones say, when you put yourself at odds with circumstance you are certain to suffer.

On this note, it's time I stopped complaining about technology, despite mixed feelings, and embrace the positive. I love the fact that the recipe for palak paneer is only a click away, that I can listen to any radio station in the world for free, that microsurgery means they can operate on the pineal tumour in my friend's brain through her nose and don't need to cut her head open. These are good things and one must rejoice in them.

*

My funny old Yorkshire man got pneumonia, went into hospital and quietly died. Now Ava lives next door. She's a retired florist, plump, with pink stripes in her hair. We share an inaugural cup of tea and ask each other questions, which is one way of getting to know people. She tells me about her failing eyesight and her three grown-up kids, one of whom has addiction issues. Two things she asks me: Where do my writing ideas come from? Why do I meditate? I give her the short answers. I get my writing ideas from life. I meditate because it helps me stay present.

The longer answers are as follows.

My writing comes my depths, my joy, my anxiety and my weird, my imagination and my interest in the stories of my tribe, who are the entire human race. It comes from the mystery of being alive, which I will never solve.

I meditate on behalf of babies yet to be born, dragonflies, dogs, musicians and gypsies. I meditate on behalf of the kid who abandoned his bicycle in the park, the girl who chucked the pregnancy kit box onto the floor of the Fremantle Railway Station toilet, the man with amputated legs slumped in his wheelchair outside the Indian cafe. I meditate to stay in touch with my own body and mind, to create a calm space in my day, to help keep the planet on an even keel.

There are many other things I could tell Ava about me. I could tell her that there was a cast, but not of thousands. There were two alcoholic parents, a three-year-old niece who died of leukaemia, a sister with a brain tumour snaking around her spine, a friend who died after being beaten up and run over by hooligans in a park. A lot of sad things happened to that dreamy girl who was me, and a lot of good things did too.

I could tell her some of the things I've done in this life: raised a son, lived in the bush, snorkelled in Samoa, written eight books, eaten plenty of fruit, been on too many committees. I could say that some nights I prefer TV to real people, which I swore I would never do. I take the phone off the hook so I can watch TV, peacefully, snug in my lavender dressing-gown. I could reveal that I'd like 'Go Girl!' to be written on my grave or 'Pencil Woman Has Gone To Heaven' or 'It was good but now it's over'. I planned to have 'She never got nor wanted a mobile phone' but then I gave in and got one.

I could mention that it's a long time since I was young but I don't feel properly old yet. How one day I was nine and then I was forty-two and suddenly I'm discussing hip operations and going to funerals. Sometimes I'm still a sulky twelve-year-old without a ready smile, or the seventeen-year-old who jumped into a bush so her boyfriend wouldn't see her dodgy haircut, a woman in her thirties juggling parenting, university and marriage, the ageing woman who tried hard to stay married but now lives alone with a moth. That I'm the sort of woman whose handbag doesn't always match her clothes and who doesn't much care. I've become my cousin: bookish, with a few stray hairs on my cardigan. I've become my grandmother who walked everywhere and lived frugally, although she was not poor. I thought I'd end up living with a bearded potter and we'd have six kids and live in the country with dogs and chooks and smoke dope, but I've become a sensible person who meditates and does yoga, sober and alone.

But I don't want to overload the poor woman, so I give her a couple of lemons and leave it at that.

> Beautiful things: A Chinese child. A cardboard box on the verge offering Free Grapefruit. The little boy in the park saying to his friend 'I won this time but you can win next time.' A ripe nectarine.

> Things that can be kept in tins: Doll's eyeballs, flower petals, marbles, lollies, buttons, pins, toenail clippings (but best not).

> Lists I haven't got around to yet: Things best done when no one's watching. Things one should not say aloud on a bus.

> Words you don't get to use very often, only one of which is made up by me: Hey nonny nonny. La-de-da. Soliloquy. Interregnum. Serendippetydoo.

Embarrassing things: Waving at someone who turns out to be a complete stranger. Attempting to put your glasses on when you already have a pair of glasses on. Trying to turn on the air conditioning with the television remote. Lighting an incense stick at the wrong end and wondering why it won't burn.

*

So, Marlena comes over to play, as promised. She's given up on RSVP and joined an international site called Planet Singles, aimed at spiritual folk with green leanings, and she's had expressions of interest from a Hindu gentlemen in Mumbai, a faded hipster in New Mexico, and a pool salesman in a nearby suburb who's learning reiki.

'I don't even know what I'm looking for,' she says wistfully. I know what she's looking for. She's looking for her husband who died. She's after a quick pathway to the warmth and love and companionship she had for all those years with him. Those days are gone, I think to myself. For although her husband died and mine left, we now inhabit the same place. Sometimes we are okay but sometimes we are wobbly. Two friends, sharing a heartache.

Nothing is more important than breakfast, nothing is more profound than lunch, as my Zen teacher says, so I dish up two bowls of Everything Soup. It's delicious. I have the urge to rename it Best Wishes Soup or perhaps Three Blessings Soup. Creative names are good. Today I am Gloria Peach Blossom, daughter of Irene Should Have Been a Poet and Bob Who Grew Vegetables.

Marlena and I drink tea, eat cake with cream, and yarn

bomb my rusty old bicycle, filling the basket with faded fake flowers I've gathered on twilight wanderings through the cemetery. Then I walk Marlena home, wheeling our rainbow bicycle to her house so it can live in her garden. We watch the latest episode of *India's Dancing Superstar*, which features dance styles from classical Bharata Natyam to krumping and robotics, with a contortionist and a very accomplished dancing dwarf thrown in for good measure. Except perhaps it is no longer correct to say dwarf? Person of shortness? Vertically challenged? Actually, Google informs me that dwarfs prefer the term 'little people', so there you go.

I stroll home in the pale evening light, admiring gardens abundant with roses, nasturtiums, wisteria, lavender and ferns. It's been a lovely day, containing all the beautiful things: art, friendship, soup and international culture.

For dinner I make a salad of green leaves, tomatoes, asparagus and fetta. I eat on my patio, watching the moon rise. Hello, elegant lemon slice of moon, I say. Hello, bright nearby star.

Then I visit Facebook, a guilty pleasure. So much of it is witless. Cutesy cats and Instagrams of alcoholic beverages are my least favourite things. (I really don't need to know how much you are drinking, people.) However, the best of it is wonderful: photographs of travelling friends, Leunig cartoons, green politics, music and art. I also check out another fave site, Humans of New York. Yay for the streets of the Big Apple, the rich variety of people, stories and outfits. Tonight I am cheered by a homeless guy who, asked what he was most proud of, replied, 'When I have extra food I feed the rats and pigeons.' You are a hero, my friend.

Preparing dinner, I examine the label of the wasabi that I'm intending to use in my salad dressing. Ingredients: hydrogenated corn syrup, water, horseradish, mustard, high fructose corn syrup, sunflower oil, soy fibre product, salt, rapeseed oil, spice extract (mustard) emulsifier (sucrose esters of fatty acids (E473), beta-cyclodextrin (E459), aluminium potassium sulphate (E522) artificial colours (FD&C Yellow 5 (E102), Blue 1 (E133)). This is even scarier than the breadcrumbs. It's not food, and I won't eat it. I try not to think about cancer, and bring to mind some happier thoughts about food. A. A. Milne: 'What I say is this: if a fellow really likes potatoes, he must be a pretty decent sort of fellow.' Spike Milligan: 'Chopsticks are one of the reasons the Chinese didn't invent custard.'

Facts are piling up, so, from my world to yours: Someone on eBay is trying to auction a potato chip in the shape of a seagull. Fingernails grow faster than toenails. An Italian brewery has teamed with a chocolate maker to create a spreadable beer product. A Tibetan mastiff recently sold in China at a luxury pet fair for two million dollars. In India six hundred million people don't have toilets. It takes fourteen rabbit skins to make an Akubra hat. There are over fifty thousand varieties of seashell.

A new day, a new day. Breakfast of tea and toast in bed, with the *New Yorker*. A review about a Guggenheim exhibition of German painting and kinetic sculpture informs me that Düsseldorf Pop still feels electric, but Düsseldorf minimalism looks tired. Glad we've got that sorted.

Someone's left a bag of apples outside my door. They're

blemished but perfect for stewing, so I make apple crumble and take some to Peta, who lives down the street. She's big, warm and talkative, and lives with her quiet husband, who works in the oil industry, and their two teenage sons. She's got a nice dog, an SUV, a swimming pool, a huge flash house, a flat-screen TV bigger than I've ever seen. She's also got cancer and she's exhausted after three weeks of chemo, with another three to go. In April she'll have both breasts cut off as a preventative measure. There's still a strong chance the cancer will return. I do my best not to offer her platitudes, and return home feeling sober. It's a tough world, Moth, I say. A very tough world.

*

What shall I write about today? I could tell you more about my early life but decide against it. My family are strange fish. All our stories put together make infinity, but I worry about which bits are mine to tell. This worrying leads to a lengthy time of staring out the window, remembering things. Moth, I ask, I wonder what will come next in this life? This seems more worthwhile than looking back into the past and mooching about it.

> What writers do instead of writing: Arrange canned goods into sweet and savoury. Clean hand basin taps with toothbrush. Think long and hard about going to Fremantle on the train to get a tattoo of a meerkat on their arm. Decide not to. Think long and hard about walking to Subiaco and getting a head of foils for $119.

Decide not to. Spend the morning shifting a comma. Spend the afternoon shifting it back again.

Oddest thing I've read recently: An Indian astrologer in Udaipur told a journalist that her chances of an inheritance were low but would increase if she fed a yellow chapati to a cow, or a yellow banana to an elephant every Thursday. If she couldn't find a cow or an elephant, she should donate yellow clothes to a charity five Thursdays in a row.

Another weird thing I read recently: In China a man has been executed for murdering a pregnant woman to sell her corpse as a ghost bride. Ghost weddings are still carried out in some areas, to prevent dead adult sons being lonely in the afterlife and thus bring misfortune to their families.

I avoid writing for a bit longer by reading a magazine article about the latest in high-tech homes, where all the functions are controlled with the swipe of a touch screen. Your bedroom has an iPod docking station connected to ceiling speakers, with a subwoofer under the bed. A flat screen hidden discreetly in the ceiling comes down at an angle so you can watch TV in bed without cricking your neck. You can even get an RFID (radio frequency identification tag) embedded in your arm so you can open the front door with a wave of your hand. Or, imagine you live somewhere ordinary but have a roof over your head, food and water and medicine, unlike seventy-five percent of the world's population. Imagine you have an old veranda, and a comfortable chair to sit on that you found by the side of the road, and some nasturtiums in the garden to look at, and some basil and parsley in a pot. Imagine you have a cup of tea to drink, imagine contentment. How come people think they need all that other shit? I seem to be angrier than I need be about this.

I cheer myself up with my favourite piece of Chinglish, which I love despite the fact that I am not sure where I came by it. Instructions that came with a pillow, perhaps, not that pillows actually need instructions. 'To improve the pattern and appearance of the product without notifying, please comprehend us. If you clip or transform the products without agreeing to the warnings, breakage and responsibility have no relationship with.'

What I would like for Christmas: World peace. A blue marble. A green silk nightgown.

Things you can write on a birthday card: Is there anything sillier than acting your age? Age does not matter, unless you are a cheese. Age and treachery will triumph over youth and skill. What if the next bit of your life was the best bit? Happy Birthday.

Poignant things: My friend running away on his tricycle, aged four, with a pile of comics in the back tray.

Fabulous people: The Dalai Lama. The autistic kid who called me Digit.

Things you shouldn't do: Eat food you don't like just because it's free.

Things you don't notice: A mouth ulcer gradually healing. Getting older.

I am still seeking a word for when your mind delivers the wrong word. This morning I was using coconut exfoliating body wash and thought, 'This smells so nice, it's a shame it's full of nasty little criminals,' when what I meant was 'This smells so nice, it's a shame it's full of nasty little chemicals.' At least I said a word that was nearly the same as the intended word, and did not try to substitute 'suitcase' or 'glove', which would have been more sinister.

My son is ruthless with me these days. 'You told me that already, Mum,' he says hastily, as I launch into a repeat. To avoid him rolling his eyeballs too much, I recount the story about an elderly man who belonged to a tribe where, when you got old and useless, they put you in a box and threw you off a cliff. As they neared the cliff edge, the man said to his son, 'Just take me out and throw me over. You might as well keep the box. They'll need it for you some day.' Reminder: Don't tell him this story again.

*

I need an outing so I walk to the shops and buy some sourdough fruit bread. The man with the sign saying he has prostate cancer is in the supermarket car park again. He works hard at it, standing under the trees for hours, in the weekends shifting to Subiaco markets. Sometimes I give him a newspaper. I wonder if he really does have prostate cancer? I asked him how his health was going once and he started talking about antibiotics which made me suspicious. I wonder why my heart is so hard about giving money to beggars? 'You're probably going to spend it on booze or drugs,' I think, and walk on, saddened by my stinginess. Sometimes I take a longer route, in order to avoid the guilt of not giving. Once, on Fifth Avenue, I offered a dreadlocked junkie peaches instead of money but it felt patronising. In Bali I gave cash to a woman, baby in her arms and kids clutching her skirt, who took it angrily, without gratitude. It was a transaction I couldn't win, if appreciation was what I was seeking. I do give money to buskers, though, if they're good. Blessings upon you, musicians of the streets.

Thing I found out today: There *is* a word for those mistakes one makes, such as "Parents scurrying around at night, trying to keep the misery/mystery of Christmas alive." It is mondegreen – a mishearing or misinterpretation of a phrase that sounds similar, which creates a new meaning.

Things I saw today: An agitated woman emerging from the shopping centre toilet, gabbling into her phone, 'I'll see you in ten seconds.' Graffiti on old station wagon: 'All the freaky people make the beauty in the world.'

I also overhear a pretty girl say to her friend, 'I look crap today, I just look crap.' I want to whisper kind words to her in a magic way that she'll hear but not find spooky, tell her not to squander her life trying to be someone a bit thinner and better looking, because it's an endless road that brings no peace.

I wasn't intending to but I drop in to Marlena's on my way home. She's sorting out her tax, which she has been threatening to do forever, but she takes a break and sits under the grapevine with me, where she shares a funny thing. Yesterday she was enjoying some afternoon self-pleasure when a courier unexpectedly knocked on her door. Flustered, she couldn't turn off her vibrator so she signed for her parcel accompanied by its weird whirring noise.

'I mumbled something about my hair dryer, but I was wearing my nightie and I was blushing. I'm sure he knew!' Who says women of a certain age have no fun. She's all excited because an interesting man has contacted her on Planet Singles. He's perfect for her: seventy, Green Left politics, loves horses and independent film and blues music. Only catch is, he lives in Tucson.

'It's madness, isn't it?' she asks. 'Even if one of us did fly halfway around the world to visit the other, it could only end badly. Either we wouldn't like each other at all, which would be dreadful ... or what if he liked me but I didn't like him, or vice versa? And if we did fall in love, then what? There's no way I'd shift to Tucson. I'd miss my grandchildren too much, and there isn't really room for cowboy Bob here in my little house ...'

'I guess there's no harm in writing to him,' I say, doubtfully. 'As long as you don't invest too much energy in it, hon.'

'Once I would have done it,' she replied. 'When I was thirty I'd have hopped on a plane and gone to meet him and trusted whatever happened next ...'

'Surely age has earned us the right to do as we please? If you want to hop on that plane, then do, and go girl you! But if this guy feels like too much hassle, just email him and untangle yourself. As the Turkish proverb goes, "No matter how far you've gone down the wrong road, turn back."'

'Thanks for listening,' says Marlena. 'Do you want some blueberries to take home for dessert?'

Back at my house I tell the moth all about it, and do some yoga in my pyjamas, smiling because someone once told me, 'It's okay to do yoga as long as you don't look yoga.' Then I watch the weather. These days they announce 'a seventy percent chance of rain' instead of forecasting rain but despite this change of approach, it usually does not rain. It just gets drier and drier. Climate change is real and it is terrifying.

Sometimes this world is too challenging for me. I'd like to live in a tree for a week. Maybe longer. Like a bird, a leaf, an angel. No longer trying to keep up with things. I'll need a new name when I live in my tree. Angel Sunday, or Infinity Mermaid. Also fruit, nuts, chocolate, water, books, a mattress, soft blankets, a lantern, a torch, something to pee in ...

In real life, it's dinnertime. I eat on my patio: fruit salad with pecans and yoghurt. Cool clear silence. A cut-in-half moon. I wash the dishes, make mint tea and take out Sei

Shōnagon's *Pillow Book* to admire her lists. In her time, apparently, men took part in the courtly practices of poetry, calligraphy, and elegance of wardrobe choice. These days certain men take part in the tedious practices of drinking too much beer and wearing pants that show their bum crack.

> Things there should be a word for: The feeling my friend had when there was a pile-up on the freeway and just before her car hit another one she thought, 'Oh, goody.' Compulsively buying wonderful art equipment that one is too scared to use.
>
> Things I've learned since my marriage ended: How to cook for one person. That it is fine to wear floral pyjama pants with a purple spotted nightshirt.
>
> Things to do on a train that require no device: Look out the window. Replace one word in a movie title with the word 'bacon': *Anne of Green Bacon*. Change one word in a book title: *Leaning towards Infinity* becomes *Lurching Towards Infinity*. Observe people. Pretend your clavicles are a big smile.
>
> Amusing T-shirts:
> I reject your reality and substitute my own.
> Six out of seven dwarves are not happy.
> Yes, I do have a truck. No, I will not help you move.
> No really. That's very interesting. Please go on.

My favourite t-shirt slogans:

Hedgehogs. Why can't they just share the hedge?

On a scale of one to ten, what is your favourite colour in the alphabet?

Everything is easier said than done. Except talking, that's about the same.

Above all else, sky.

I can't brain today. I have the dumb.

I don't have a short attention span I just... hey, look at that squirrel.

Paddle faster. I hear banjos.

Tonight's facts: In 1932, Peg Entwistle, a failed movie actress aged twenty-four, jumped to her death from the H of Hollywood. Finnish children celebrate Easter by dressing up with scarves around their heads, painting their faces, and taking to the streets armed with coffeepots and bunches of twigs. The European Union's regulations on the sale of cabbages is 26,911 words long, while the Ten Commandments is 179 words. A nerve impulse in the brain can travel 274 kilometres an hour. There's a worm called a bone-eating snot flower.

*

Next day. I take my camera to be fixed but am told it is Beyond Economical Repair, which is a polite way of saying it's screwed. Shame. Marlena and I go curb crawling, AKA verge shopping. One of the advantages of living in a posh suburb is the things wealthy people chuck out. Marlena scores two floral rugs and I find some Italian magazines, a terracotta pot, and two ties with elephants on them. My nephew loves all things elephant, in case you think I am just plain potty. Don't answer that. Marlena is quieter than usual, but she seems happy enough. When we get tired of hunting and gathering we sit in the park admiring the roses. Marlena heads off so I go to the library, then come home and cook a nice piece of salmon for lunch. Ava comes by and tells me she's fighting with her daughter-in-law again. Her son has a drug problem and she keeps giving him money and wondering why he doesn't return her phone calls. 'How's that working for you?' I want to ask. Doctor Phil asks people that. It's a good question. However, I remind myself that trying to fix other people is unwise so I just listen and hug her as she leaves. Do some mending, pot some geraniums, and am settling down to watch *Antiques Road Show* when Marlena rings.

'I'm going. I've decided. I'm tired of being cautious. I've been cautious all my life. Could be two weeks of wonderful, but if not, I'll stay in a motel and explore the delights of Tucson.'

I'm grinning when I get off the phone. Everyone says 'carpe diem' but not many people actually do it. Risk is a scary thing, but it is also a wonderful thing. All mysteries will eventually be solved. The knife you lost will turn up days later under the toaster. The day you die will arrive and take you by surprise. What will count is all the adventures you've had, not your hesitations and regrets. Here's to Marlena, Moth, I say. Here's to fun!

*

Suddenly it's December and the festive season is upon me. I get out the gifts I've gathered: books, candles in old teacups, colourful aprons, and tra la la, plus cards and wrapping paper, and start to wrap. Halleluiah! For who can truly hate Christmas? It's a fine time of year if you don't get sucked into consumerism, perfectionism or any other dreadfulism. Celebrate simply, quietly, gently. If it all gets too much, take to the beach, the park, the forest, your bed. Savour the joyous moments, the cars with reindeer ears, the tiny fairy lights.

> Wonderful signs I've seen outside houses: 'Galileo was born here'. 'In this house nothing exciting ever happened and no one famous ever lived here.'

> More good words you don't get to use very often: Nudiustertian: of or relating to the day before yesterday. Ugsome: dreadful, loathsome. Purlieu: a neighbouring area. Frustraneous: useless or unprofitable.

> Good things to do: Wear your best clothes every day. Detach from drama.

> Unavoidable things: Taxes. Death. Grot in kitchen drawers. Bad weather. Relatives. Dentistry. The ten thousand joys and ten thousand sorrows.

Facts for the Year's End: In Melbourne there are 18,000 homeless people. Australians spend fourteen billion dollars on alcohol annually, and ten billion on beauty-related products. Yoyos were once banned in Damascus because it was believed they were causing a drought. A Balinese traditional healing treatment may include deep-tissue massage, being poked with sharp sticks, and having chewed herbs spat at you. King Frederick the Great of Prussia drank coffee made with champagne. It's illegal to drink beer out of a bucket sitting on a curb in St. Louis. Leonardo Da Vinci could draw with one hand and write with the other hand at the same time. Human beings have two fewer chromosomes than a potato.

I've written my way towards you, written about the small things that make up a life. New Year's Eve. I stand on my balcony watching fireworks blazing in the night, far away above the river. Here in the angel house of god, I farewell the year. I put roses on my shrine, beside the heart-shaped rock and the three lady Buddhas. I dedicate my offering to the salvation of our ailing planet, to the wellbeing of every living thing. Here I am then, the late-at-night-lady who loves cherries. Holy holy holy, joyous and alive.

Occasions that induce
HALF-HEARTEDNESS

THINGS THAT MAKE YOU FEEL
NOSTALGIC

Things that make you feel cheerful

REFINED AND ELEGANT THINGS

Topics of poetry

THINGS THAT
CREATE A DISTURBANCE

Things that just keep passing by

ON Zen AND Creativity

Zen and Creativity

I have no bowl. I accept it with two hands. Ozaki Hōsai

I met Buddhism in my twenties and have never wavered in knowing it is the path for me. My exploration of the fundamental teaching – that all phenomena are impermanent, unsatisfactory and not-self – continues to unfold and deepen. After many years of meditation and study in the Theravada tradition, my spiritual practice grew stale. In search of a fresh approach, I stumbled across Zen. I loved the simplicity, the elegant rituals, the silence interspersed with bells. Yet despite twenty-five years of sitting zazen, the practice continues to challenge and surprise. Koans mystify me. Daily sitting, alone with my restless mind, is often a struggle, yet I have a deep and steadfast love of the Great Way. It seems my heart knows something my brain does not. The rigours of a seven-day sesshin, with its early rising and long, weary hours of meditation, are deeply challenging, yet afterwards I feel alive and at peace with myself and the world. Despite my restless mind and my strong resistance, the hard work of sitting takes me deeper into original mind. Everything opens up. Tastes and smells become more vivid, merriment finds its way into my life and my writing.

Zen and creativity have a long and ancient history. In the thirteenth century Zen travelled from China to Japan. It realised itself in the new culture in many forms, including calligraphy, brush painting, haiku, ceramics, bamboo flute, gardening, ikebana, and the tea ceremony. The sitting practice of zazen is one aspect of Zen training. The other is practising the discipline of an art form to deepen one's understanding. One might consider one's creative life and one's spiritual life to be separate but we have only have one life, and in it everything resides. Nothing is left out. No separation. All things are intimately linked, not only in ancient times but right here, right now, in our messy busy moments. As Clarissa Pinkola Estes points out, the creative life itself is a spiritual practice. How this evolves is different for each of us. For Diane Ackerman, writing is a form of inquiry, as well as a site of celebration and prayer. Natalie Goldberg used to ask her teacher endless questions about her Zen practice, not understanding his answers. 'But Roshi ...' she would reply, mystified. In the end he explained things to her by saying, 'Natalie, like in your writing,' allowing her to see that at a profound level, her writing *was* her practice.

There is no map for the direction one's spiritual or artistic life will take. However hard we try to control or predict outcomes, things are far more dangerous and interesting than that. Zen requires us to trust the present moment, and respond to it from our depths. Creativity asks the same thing. Whether you are a painter, a sculptor, a musician or a writer, the road will involve mistakes, dry spells and total surrender to the way things are. You will have to stay current and give up your fancy notions, your fantasies, your preferences.

Zen demands you go deeper into everything, into the sounds around you, into the wild landscape of your body. Can you be fully present for each passing moment: the comfort of a hug, the fragrance of a mango? How does fear taste when you read about someone running over their child? How does anger manifest when a driver yells abuse at you at the end of a hard day? Zen, like art, calls us to attention. It asks us to slow down, to allow, to be still. Gardens, kitchens, blank paper, coloured pencils, fabrics, piano keys, broken crockery ... what might become of them, in your open hands?

Ram Dass says, 'Every religion is the product of the conceptual mind attempting to describe the Mystery,' and perhaps all art is the product of the conceptual mind responding to the Mystery, but Zen is more enigmatic than that. It asks us to forget the conceptual mind and respond from a place beyond words. It demands a unique, personal response to this world of a thousand joys and a thousand sorrows and those thousand emails you don't feel like answering. Creativity, too, is a path you forge in ways entirely your own, whether it involves decorating a cake, drawing an elephant, or writing a song.

'We are all sculptors and painters, and our material is our own flesh and blood and bones,' said Thoreau. In artistic life everything is useful; nothing is left out. Scraps of fabric from old clothing become a quilt, limp vegies in your fridge become a soup, the thought or image that haunts you becomes a haiku.

It's not about perfection. The door marked 'good' sticks, as the Chinese proverb warns. I love this story of a young man learning the art of gardening from an old monk. The apprentice worked hard for many hours, weeding, clearing leaves and raking sand until the garden was immaculate, but when the old master came to inspect it, he frowned. Then he shook the tree so that the cherry blossoms fell on the path.

Like that!

We often think of Zen as a practice of stillness but the other half of mature spiritual practice is expression. Nothing stands in isolation, each of us is part of a wider community. Neither Zen nor creativity is a solitary path, although at times they may seem that way. A cartoon, a painting, a flower arrangement, a piece of writing, is a gift, it takes its place in the world and in the hearts and minds of those who come across it. Individual spiritual and artistic practices are offered for their own sake, and this blossoming also serves to illuminate fellow travellers.

Creativity can take many forms. Sometimes it is a form of protest, a personal response to the greed, hatred and ignorance arising endlessly in the world around us. A concert about ruined pianos can be, amongst other things, a poignant and instructive response to what white Australians have done to the indigenous people of this land. Photographs of a footprint and a discarded plastic sample bag littering the moon's surface are a political response to the devastation mankind wreaks on every corner of the universe. In the hands of sculptors, decommissioned guns become musical instruments. Art can amuse, delight, inspire and challenge. Zen practice can be done alone on a black cushion; it can also be done on the streets, in community, in galleries and performance spaces.

John Daido Loori says that the Zen arts were created to communicate the essential wordlessness of Zen. This is a paradox perhaps, but Zen and life are full of paradoxes. Hakuin Ekaku, the great Zen master who revived the Rinzai tradition, stated that words are nothing but an overflow of delusion. Yet words express our deepest loves and deepest sorrows, so we line up letters into words and sentences, and set them free into the universe, where they belong to nobody and everyone.

I love haiku, the ancient and deceptively simple poetic form in which the use of so few words conveys so much. Seifu, a Zen nun, wrote this in the sixteenth century:

> The faces of dolls
> In unimaginable ways
> I must have grown old

Bashō, on death:

> Dying cricket –
> how full of
> life, his song.

Haiku were traditionally bound by strict rules governing not only form but subject matter. For example, in renga, which are a series of linked haiku, a peony or a dragonfly could be mentioned only once in every hundred verses. The four seasons, the natural world, death and mountains were common topics but in modern times, haiku address more everyday affairs, like this one by Seiun:

At the ticket window
Our child becomes
One year younger.

Haiku are not easy to write. The more condensed the form, the more difficult the task. They are language squeezed tight, meaning written large. Here, as in all art forms, the Zen aesthetic avoids the phoney and the fancy. The aim is for what Gary Snyder calls 'the weave that produces an elegant plainness.'

Seido Ray Ronci, an American Rinzai Zen monk and a poet, says that for him, poetry has always been a practice in and of itself. It's not only the practice of using language, it is also a practice of being aware: of being absorbed by each moment. When he paints, or plays piano, he tries to remove himself completely, letting the painting paint itself, the song play itself, the poem write itself. It then becomes what the words want to say, not what he wants to say, which he believes comes from silence.

It's late at night. What an earth was I thinking, taking on a topic this big? I drink camomile tea, muck around on the net, chance upon a video of Max Gimblett in his New York loft, his strong, hairy arms smudged with red and black paint. I love this guy, an internationally acclaimed painter whose Zen practice informs his work with great authenticity. He lays down a large sheet of rice paper, takes a huge brush, dips it in thick black ink. With one swift expressive stroke, he paints an enzo, the circle symbolic of everything and nothing, the universe and the void. 'Empty your mind and let it come from your body. Let it come,' he instructs. Serious political statement, talk of death, laughter and play, all have a place in that circle. When you treat life as a cosmic adventure, not a problem to be fixed, there is room for magic, for mischief, for the marvellous. As Kobi Yamada says, 'everything is a once-in-a-lifetime experience,' or in Ross Bolleter's words, 'all of this for a short time only.' It's now and one day it will be never. Zen and the creative life, each demand your original response to this moment. One chance, one encounter.

You don't have to call yourself anything or stick with only one art form. We are dancers as well as writers, musicians as well as fathers. Life is richer and more wonderful than we can possibly imagine, once we venture beyond the known and into original mind, coming forth to delight in the fertility of existence, and its expression. Zazen, a lifelong sitting practice, is the foundation stone. From that solid ground, we learn to 'rest in the place that the next line of the poem comes from, or the next note of the musical composition, or the next brush stroke', as Zen teacher John Tarrant suggests.

Along with writing, cooking is my Zen practice. I learned to cook when I was twelve years old. My mother didn't get home from work until late so she gave me a small food budget and the job of preparing dinner. Clueless, I spent most of the money on magazines. At first my meals were dreadful, burnt chops and lumpy mashed potatoes, but

I gradually improved, making it up as I went along. Later, living in a Buddhist community, I learned to cook for large numbers, transforming basic ingredients into tasty meals, working with what was to hand. These days I prepare food as a practice, bringing joy to the task. On Mondays I'm a housekeeper, making meals for a wealthy family but it's not merely a job, done by rote for money. In Dogen's essay 'Tenzo Kyōkun' ('Instructions for the Cook') he says that to cook for someone is not just to prepare food, it is to express your sincerity. When shopping, I respond to the seasons, choosing vegetables carefully, considering flavours and textures. Maybe a plump aubergine, basil from my garden, feta, or perhaps haloumi?

Before I cook, I bow to those who planted and harvested the food, in gratitude to the people who drove the truck, packed the shelf, stood at the checkout all day. I bow in honour those who go hungry, remembering that many of the world's population don't have access to plentiful food, water or shelter. I chop mindfully, breathing into my belly when I'm tired. Each part of the task is important. Taking out the rubbish, I savour the late afternoon breeze. It's very simple. I love people. I love apricots and avocadoes and herbs. Cooking nourishes me, as well as the world, and a kitchen offers endless opportunity for creativity and delight.

Ways to come forth, not just in our silent practice on the cushion but in our lives, are many and various. Why waste them? Why squander our precious time? By our efforts we bring relevance into our lives. We attend fully to this one moment, that contains all moments. We allow the ordinary to enliven us.

Perhaps the last word should go to Michael Leunig in his cartoon, 'The Deficit': 'Mr Curly owes much to his teapot. It has given him a lot. He is in debt to the moon and the stars. His debt to the birds is huge. For the joy they have given him he owes much to the trees and flowers. To the table, the chair, the cat, the dog, the vase, the mandolin, the duck, he owes a large debt. Can he ever repay? Well of course he can! That's the whole point of his life.'

Jive

in the slow dance of morning   in the strange depths of night
in the blessing of fleets   in the making of arrangements
zen meets my life
in the squashed face of the moon
in my desire to go to antarctica
wearing a blue chenille dressing-gown
in the impossibility of writing a perfect poem about a pear
while mending my clothes   while chopping coriander
while buying a book
in the midst of a traffic jam in a wild sunset a small surprise
a belly laugh & a mug of ginger tea
as i peer into my letterbox   buy an airline ticket
send a postcard
they disappear into each other
surrendering to silence or singing along
summer autumn winter spring
plain brown wrapper or tissue paper with flowers
flimsy as a dragonfly wing strong as gold mountain
rolling along like an old milky marble
up down & all over the place & nowhere to be found
in the land of the eternal breadboard, the glass rose
the electric sandshoe & the sacred dental floss
zen meets my life

The Zen Cook

She is boiling the rice and frying an onion.
She smells of coriander and coffee, vanilla and sweat.
She is the cake mother and the porridge queen,
the pancake tosser, the tofu goddess,
the sifter of all the flours.
She says
a raisin is not a shrivelled grape,
a raisin is a sweet brown dancer of sun and earth,
a raisin is the belly button of god.
She raises her glass.
She carves a turnip into a rose.
She is standing in her kitchen, laughing,
pointing a radish at the moon.

Apricot

I am walking across a field.

I am walking across a field eating a sweet summer apricot.

I am walking across a field eating a sweet summer apricot thinking about my life and wondering what to do with it.

I am walking across a field eating a sweet summer apricot thinking about my life and wondering what to do with it and contemplating changes like maybe losing weight and getting a proper job.

I am walking across a field eating a sweet summer apricot thinking about my life and wondering what to do with it and contemplating changes like maybe losing weight and getting a proper job and finding a new therapist and learning printmaking.

I am walking across a field eating a sweet summer apricot thinking about my life and wondering what to do with it and contemplating changes like maybe losing weight and getting a proper job and finding a new therapist and learning printmaking and giving up dairy products.

I am walking across a field eating a sweet summer apricot thinking about my life and wondering what to do with it and contemplating changes like maybe losing weight and getting a proper job and finding a new therapist and learning printmaking and giving up dairy products and going to live in the country.

I am walking across a field eating a sweet summer apricot thinking about my life and wondering what to do with it and contemplating changes like maybe losing weight and getting a proper job and finding a new therapist and learning printmaking and giving up dairy products and going to live in the country and learning the names of all the birds.

I am walking across a field eating a sweet summer apricot thinking about my life and wondering what to do with it and contemplating changes like maybe losing weight and getting a proper job and finding a new therapist and learning printmaking and giving up dairy products and going to live in the country and learning the names of all the birds and rereading all the French feminists, when I decide it might be easier not to bother with any of it.

I am walking across a field eating a sweet summer apricot.

Elegant Sufficiency

When I visited Samoa, I stayed in a *fale*, a simple structure, basically a tent on a platform. Because it had no shelves or hooks, small finds became important. Two pegs were bounty, as was a coat hanger. Now I could peg my towel on the line and hang up my dress. In Bali, a young man showed me the room where he and his wife lived. It fronted a communal courtyard and contained a bed, a toilet, a rice cooker, crockery and a clothes rack. In a village in Ireland I glanced into a doorway to see a fireplace, an armchair, a table and a teapot. The basic requisites of life are few. In my own small apartment, I do my best to live minimally but there's plenty of stuff I don't need.

Living simply isn't new to me. My parents were bohemians. Our household was short on money but we lived well. Our house was decorated with paintings given by artist friends, and flowers from our garden. My sisters and I wore good clothes which were hand-me-downs and jumble sale finds. Endlessly resourceful, my mother embroidered bright woollen flowers around the moth holes in our cardigans. We ate delicious meals of homegrown vegetables, cheap cuts of meat cooked slowly and given flavour with herbs and spices. Visitors brought seafood and wine. After school we drank freshly squeezed grapefruit juice, and ate carrot sticks or nuts and raisins. Outings were the beach, the library or the local pool. A theatre visit or a film was a rare treat. My mother was the queen of creative. She'd unfold a chicken noodle soup packet to make a small book, on whose two silvery pages you could write a story with a ball point pen. She made her own wholemeal bread, giving me a lump of dough, to fashion a bread girl with raisin eyes. I made puppets out of old socks, paper dolls from magazine pictures, cubby houses from blankets and armchairs. There were always things to do that didn't cost any money.

What we learn in childhood informs our adult lives. I still love creating with glue, paint, scissors, scraps of this and that. I made my granddaughter's teaset using a teapot and tiny coffee cups from an op shop, rather than buying a new pink plastic one. When she's old enough I hope she'll want to make paper dolls and bread people with me. I hunt and gather when there are council collections, reinventing items found on the roadside. I blend my own hummus and buy tomatoes when they're cheap, roasting them with oil and balsamic vinegar, rather than buying designer items. I walk in parks, take the train, and live as simply as I can. I don't feel deprived. I feel content.

I've always found making and mending satisfying, yet I live in a capitalist culture where having more stuff is supposed to bring more happiness. The imperative to work harder and consume more is deeply ingrained, and fed by fear of lack. Having possessions isn't a bad thing. We are human. We like to make nests, to collect things, but too much stuff is too much stuff and the planet can no longer support our greed. It is easy to agree to this premise but harder to walk the talk of it. Making conscious choices to live in a leaner way does not mean deprivation. A simple life can be rich and full and creative. It involves knowing what is enough. It means celebrating what you have, and slowing down enough to savour the good stuff.

Voluntary simplicity feels right to me but it's a practice, not a fixed position. I'm still learning the difference between wanting and needing. Dipa Ma was a Bangladeshi sage who lived in a tiny flat in Calcutta. When she came to America to teach meditation, one of her observations was that you don't need nine types of tea. The cultural message that we are not enough and that we don't have enough is pervasive and insidious. Some days I think people would love me more if I wore more expensive shoes. At times I crave cheap, colourful crap from the Red Dot shop but the planet pays a high price for the one dollar bucket, the five dollar t-shirt. In Beijing there are over sixty days a year where the air quality is so poor that schools don't let children play outside. We are all losers if our bargains cost other people the right to breathe clean air. Before you buy something, ask these questions: Is it necessary? Is it sustainable? Will it satisfy me?

Abundance is a state of mind. We already have all the conditions for our own happiness. If we don't curb our wanting and hurry to the next wanting, satisfaction is bypassed and replaced by further wanting. In the extreme, compulsive shoppers often don't even unwrap what they have bought, they just head off and buy something else. In my own case, I notice how I'm prone to wolfing down a meal, scarcely tasting it, in order to hurry towards another serving.

In Tibetan Buddhism it is said that to maintain mindfulness as long as it takes to drink a cup of tea accumulates more merit than years of practising generosity, discipline and asceticism. To just be present, and feel satisfied, when eating or drinking tea, is a very high art.

Let us be content with what we have. Let us not be consumed by our addiction to more. Let us not be hungry ghosts in this lifetime.

In the World

in the strange early morning half light we sit
in the cloudiness of our questioning we sit
in our madness and our clarity we sit
in the midst of too much to do we sit
in the warm arms of our shared sorrow we sit
in community and in loneliness we sit
in sweet exhaustion we sit
in the blazing energy of being alive we sit

here with the singing crickets
here with each electric birdsong
here with the rippling of breezes and the dry grasses
here with the cobwebs and the clouds
and the dusty road upon us

us in the sound and the sound in us

us in the world and the world in us

Things that should be

big

THINGS THAT SHOULD BE SMALL

Things that create a disturbance

THINGS THAT NO ONE NOTICES

Things that are hard on the ear

THINGS THAT ARE BETTER AT NIGHT

ON Writing

Slow Train

In 2008, I started an essay about writer's block.

I'd begun my writing career by returning to university when I was thirty-five, after years of doing every other possible thing. It was wonderful, talking about ideas and hanging out with other misfits. I did the assignments, got good grades, a pertinent comment or two. My poetry and semi-autobiographical short fiction won prizes. Now I was a writer. With no goal in mind beyond the payment of three thousand dollars I wrote a young adult book for the Dolly Fiction series. It wasn't hard, so when I left university I wrote *Guitar Highway Rose*, a more quirky creative YA book that became a bestseller. An agent had knocked back my collection of short fiction, saying it was unpublishable and looked like it had been written in a writing class. Mortified, I followed the money and concentrated on work for which there was a market. Fifteen years later I'd written seven books for teenagers. I enjoyed doing it for most of that time, and I built a solid career: appearances at writers festivals, workshops in schools, teaching at university, awards, residencies. It looked enviable, from the outside.

But I was over it. I didn't want to write for teenagers any longer but I wasn't sure what to do next. I was in my fifties.

I was restless. My marriage was crumbling, although I hadn't admitted it yet, so I composed a convincing grant application, saying I wanted to change genres and rework the semi-autobiographical adult novel I had written for my MA, and I was granted a prestigious fellowship, the Buddle Findlay Sargeson.

There was a big fuss, a fancy awards ceremony at Government House, with chamber music, crisp champagne and elegant speeches. So there I was, in early autumn, living by myself in a studio apartment near Auckland University. A photographer from the *Sunday Times* took a photograph of me, leaning against the ivy-clad wall in my black and white dress, trying to look intelligent. I had high hopes for myself. So did everyone else.

But God laughs at our plans, as they say, and this became more and more evident as the months wore on. Firstly, I faced a major problem with the roof. When the rains began, so did the leaking. I spent hours phoning the committee and the plumber, and mopping floods of water from beneath my bed. When my husband flew in to visit, the poor weary fellow left his bag on the airport bus. We borrowed a car and went in search of his bag, returning to find I'd locked us out of the apartment. We broke in with the aid of a homeless man and a wheelie bin. Things went downhill from there. It would be fair to say it was not a successful visit.

The weeks slipped by. I watched the passing students from my window, so young, so seemingly carefree. I bought cheap fruit and vegetables at the Chinese grocery on Karangahape Road. Auckland was my home town, although I hadn't lived there for decades, so I spent time with friends and family. I sat in the library and read, and I mopped my flooded floor.

I couldn't write a fucking thing.

I could hardly bear to look at my novel. I began several short stories, none of which had legs. I wrote a few lines of poetry. I read so much about writer's block it was coming out of my ears, but my essay went no further than other people's thoughts, gathered from library books and the internet, and random jottings.

The article I liked most claimed there's no such thing as writer's block. Instead, one of three things might be happening.

One. You can't write because you're dealing with a major life event such as a health issue or the death of a beloved. Once this is dealt with, your writing will flow.

Two. Your work has a technical problem. Your story is in the first person but would work better in the third person, or you need to do more research. Define the problem. Fix it, seeking advice if need be.

Three. Your well has run dry. Take a break. Feed your soul. Nourish your creativity. Inspiration will return.

This theory may be overly simple, but it has some validity. If you aren't writing, those are plausible reasons.

In my case, it was no wonder I was blocked, as all three applied. My marriage was on the slippery slope. My novel was a structural nightmare that began well, got worse, then tailed off into nowhere. My years of writing books one after another had left me depleted. Add a leaky roof, the hefty responsibility of the fellowship, plus a tendency to melancholy. I was doomed. I wrote in my notebook: *I haven't written anything for so long my fingers are stuck to my skull and the ink in me is almost invisible.* Whether you call it writer's block or not, nothing of literary value was produced during that time. It wasn't because I didn't try. It was because I couldn't. Deeply ashamed, I went back to my life, for a while, and wrote one more YA book.

There are many hypotheses about writer's block. I won't go into all of them. I like what Tobias Hill says, though, which is that nine tenths of his writing is really thinking and thinking takes time. Perhaps you are not blocked, you just need to relax and give yourself permission to do your thinking. Jungians suggest the psyche has its own seasons and that fallow times are a necessary part of the creative process. Again this provides a measure of truth. Who knows what is bubbling away inside us, and when it will decide to make its way out of our murky darkness? It takes a measure of faith, however, to live with this ambiguity and trust that the writing will return in its own good time.

But here's what I actually believe about this whole thing. Stick with me now. I once told my friend Mari Rhydwen how stuck I can get on a small decision. The example I gave was wanting to buy myself flowers, but standing frozen outside the shop, dithering. Her advice was this. Buy the flowers and enjoy them. Or walk away and forget about them completely. The two worst things you can do are to not buy them and spend all afternoon wishing you had, or buy them and then agonise about how you couldn't really afford them and how buying treats will not fill your inner emptiness and how you are really a very neurotic person and how come you have no money in the bank and no one loves you.

My point is this. Either write, or don't write.

If you are not writing, don't write. Stop! Fully and completely. Accept the fact that you can't be bothered, that you would rather watch *The Big Bang Theory* or go to Ikea. Do this without guilt or punishment. You are not a pasta machine. You'll only turn out poor quality work if you force yourself onwards, grudging and unwilling. Plus you'll be miserable. Old or young, we are all on our last cruise, as Robert Louis Stevenson put it, so why make yourself do something you really don't want to do. These days, when I don't want to write, I surrender to that. I idle and moodle, walk, cook, rest, draw, paint or sew, go to the art gallery, to the beach, to a movie.

Who'd be a writer, anyway? James Joyce said that each one of us starts out as a poet and then realises it's too hard. The same can be said about all writing. It's sedentary, lonely, boring and physically demanding. Additionally, there isn't any money in it these days, except for a few authors at the top. Book sales are down, advances are rare, print runs are small. Recently I heard publishing referred to as 'a sunset industry.' You'd be better off financially to train as a florist, an architect, a barista, just about anything else.

Furthermore, if you have nothing to say, it's wise to say nothing. Many writers stopped after one or two good books. Some other writers should have. There are those who wrote well in the beginning but whose work got steadily weaker. I was once at a book launch where someone said about the elderly, well-known writer, 'Lovely fellow, pity about the writing.' So, if you have published a few things but are now struggling endlessly, why not stop now, while the going is good? As J. D. Salinger famously said, there is a great peace in not publishing. Your life will be much less stressful if you give it up forever.

But, you say, I'm unconvinced by your argument. I have idled long enough. I'm sick of making marmalade and watching old movies. Like Harold Pinter, when I can't write I feel like some part of myself is banished. Of its own accord, the muse has returned to me. I have an urge to write poetry, to begin a new play, song, film script. It is as if the fairies removed the names of everything but now I must ink my way back to them. I've remembered why I love writing. I am a person who delights in words. I collect them. I love them, as Pablo Neruda does: 'Words / as slippery as smooth grapes, / words exploding in the light'.

In that case, forget barista or postman.

WRITE.

Write with every ounce of your being. Write as if your hair is on fire. Be the writing. Apply yourself to what Owen Marshall calls 'the necessary strict toiling with language.' Don't wait until tomorrow, next week, after Christmas. There's no perfect time to write. There's only now. You want to be a writer. Okay. Stop whingeing about how hard it is. 'Work with pleasure only,' as Henry Miller advised. Stop being a lazy bugger. Show up for work everyday and give it everything you've got.

THINGS THAT WON'T HELP.

Don't go into bookshops. It will make you feel that every book has already been written. Instead, go to an Italian greengrocer and fondle the tomatoes. Browse in a homewares shop, even though you will never buy a fragrant candle for one hundred dollars and you don't need another pair of earrings. While away an hour in a cafe that brews good tea. Now go back to your desk and write like stink.

Don't talk about it too much, or even at all. Shirley Hazzard refuses to discuss her current writing. 'If I talk about it I hear a voice inside me saying "Now you have destroyed everything."' Remember the ancient Chinese saying: Talk won't cook rice.

Don't expect perfection. 'Just vomit out a first draft,' as Nora Roberts suggests. It works for her because she's written 209 romance novels. Write something, anything. Later you can fix it, rearrange it, embroider, polish, perfect. Every writer faces the fact that, as Balzac said, it is as easy to dream a book as it is hard to write one. There will be an alarming gap between the vision splendid and the useless mess on the page. However, keep going. Include everything, your impulses, your nervy restlessness, your urgencies, your delights and despairs. This is how a book gets written. You start something with a lot of hope. It goes wrong. You complain to your friends, you eat too much, you wish you'd married someone rich and lived in Mauritius. Keep going. Somehow you will rescue it. If you have to be perfect, if you stop because of that, you are screwed. Even when you don't know where you are going, go there. Trust that.

GOOD TRICKS, OR THINGS THAT MIGHT HELP.

Once you have decided to write, avoid email and Facebook. They squander your time greedily, relentlessly. Check them once a day, as briefly as possible. If you are really addicted, you might consider purchasing Freedom, a blocking program that forcibly deactivates wi-fi connections for set periods.

Be very clear about what is it you want to say. Don't write clever rubbish. If it's technically brilliant but contains no news from the soul, there's no point in saying it. Your job is to say things that have not yet been said. Martin Amis suggests that all writing should be 'a campaign against cliché. Not just clichés of the pen but of the mind and heart.'

Say no to almost everything people invite you to, or ask you to do. In the words of Charles H. Spurgeon, 'Learn to say No. It will be of more use to you than to be able to read Latin.' This buys you time, which you need. Writing is long, slow patience and it's necessary to put in the hours. You will feel ruthless and mean and deeply alone but don't weaken. People will try to seduce you. Poet Saradha Koirala was invited by friends to 'Come with us now and you can write a poem about it later.'

Introverts quite like being rigorously anti-social. Extroverts may benefit from going out gallivanting. Trust your own process. If you do say yes, make sure it is a yes worth saying. Don't hang out with the tedious. Once you have bought yourself time, use it well. There's no point saying you're busy then spending the evening tidying your linen cupboard.

Reread your notebooks. Who knows what you will find

there? Poet Audre Lorde had a year in which everything went violently wrong: health, love life, job. She scribbled crazy self-indulgent weird stuff in her journal, not in the service of great literature but in order to save her own life. Later, rereading, she found the bones of a poetry collection. Take all those factoids you have collected and see what you can do with them. One day I'll find a use for mine. *André Breton said that the man who cannot visualise a horse galloping on a tomato is an idiot. The Japanese have a word, age-otori, which means 'people who look worse after a haircut.' Leonardo da Vinci invented a machine that would wake you up by tickling your feet.*

Google Writer's Block. This will keep you amused for ages. It's reassuring to know that Martin Amis describes writing as a boring, nose-picking, arse-scratching job and that Junot Diaz says that if you don't feel lost when writing a novel it means you're in a place someone has been before. Don't spend too long doing this. Half hour max. Eat lunch, something healthy like mushrooms on toast and a piece of fruit, then back to work.

You have to be prepared to stay home in baggy, unflattering clothing, restless and edgy. For only, say, a year or two. One needs a high tolerance for frustration and lots of patience. I have never met a writer who had either of those. We are a moody, anxious, neurotic lot who prefer furtive eating, daydreaming, talking on the telephone and generally buggering around. If temporarily stuck, ask yourself if what you are doing is keeping you in energy and flow? If not, why not? Go back to those three reasons, perhaps.

Forget lofty goals. Forget competitions, grants, fame,

money, how to get an agent. First you have to write something. That's all, write something. The other stuff follows later. Just be in your life. Taste a wild storm, a slow day, a slice of papaya. Enjoy yourself. Eat your breakfast, have a shower, then sit down, plain and simple, and write a page or two.

Look after yourself. Writing is a long haul, and you won't make the distance if you neglect your body. Make self-care a priority. Eat properly and stay off the booze. Get enough sleep. You must learn to be regular and orderly in your life so that you may be violent and original in your work, as Flaubert advised. Inhabit your body, not just your brain. Swim, dance, do yoga, lie down on the floor with your feet up the wall to rest your back. 'You only have to let the soft animal of your body / love what it loves', as Mary Oliver writes in her poem 'Wild Geese'. Honour the body's basic needs. Walking is good. Hippocrates called it man's best medicine. I have never met a writer who didn't do plenty of walking.

Encourage silence. Take a day on which you do everything at half speed, do less, do as little as possible, do nothing at all. How long is it since you read all day? Or sat by a lake, watching ducks? These things will feed you, and feed your work. Practise the art of quiet.

Accept that while you are writing, you may not be able to earn much money. Some people can. They have a well-paid day job and six lovely children and they get up at 4am to write for two hours every morning. We hate those people. Find some way, your own way, to buy yourself time for writing. Learn to love things that are free: library books, lentils, the beach. As Mary Oliver says, 'One can live simply and honourably on just about enough money to keep a chicken alive', if one is willing.

Trust the process. Sue Woolfe once wrote seven kilos of untamed material she had no idea what to do with. She knew how much it weighed because she posted it all to herself in Greece. Undaunted, she underlined all the bits about an ugly woman with one highlighter, the bits about a beautiful woman with another. The parts about landscape she highlighted in green. An architecture began to present itself, and the characters came to life. Her prize-winning novel *Leaning Towards Infinity* is testament to keeping at it even when you don't know where you are headed.

Give yourself small goals and rewards. Apparently Lady Gregory, who was William Butler Yeats' patron, wouldn't let him socialise with other houseguests until he had written six lines of poetry. Have fun with this. When I finish this tricky bit, I will put on some music and dance. If I work all day today, I can go out to play tomorrow. Over to you.

Don't let fear and anxiety run your show. Turn up the corner of your mouth and smile. Try to stay in your happy place. It's all a mad circus. One day you'll be dead and none of it will matter. Let the small amusements be amusing. Put your dread, your neurosis, your poor self-esteem to one side, and keep writing.

Kafka said 'simply wait'. Well yes, but don't spend too long waiting. Books don't write themselves, you know. You have to put glue on your arse and do the work.

Accept that writing will take something from you. D. H. Lawrence said he preferred painting to writing, it cost the soul a lot less. A favourite *New Yorker* cartoon of mine is of a couple in a restaurant. The woman asks the man, 'William, do you have the courage to love?' Do you have the courage to write?

In my own case, this is what happened. My husband left me. I left New Zealand. I fell to bits completely. I didn't imagine I'd ever write again. The irony was that my book, *Juicy Writing: Inspiration and Techniques for Young Writers*, was selling well and inspiring writers of all ages. (It's a great book and still in print, so please buy it. Support this ailing industry. Also, I need to buy some lentils.)

You will have to find your own way. But don't expect to be creative a-go-go all the time, I'd written in the chapter about being stuck. I wasn't expecting to be creative a-go-go, but I wasn't expecting to spend months in a psych ward either. They were hard yards but when I returned to the land of nearly normal, I went to a doll-making workshop with textile artist Nalda Searles. Playing with colours and fabrics and threads loosened something in me. I felt the urge to write creeping back again. 'The needle is a great pen,' commented Nalda. Another journal note, from that time: *Climbing a broken staircase built of words, unsteady, out of the basement of my despair*.

Two other things helped me find my way back to my writing.

'Even if you never write anything again, you're still a good writer, Mum,' said my son. His faith in me helped me find some faith in myself.

The other thing was reading Helen Garner's book, *The Feel of Steel*, a wonderful collection, honest and sad, about the end of her third marriage, in which she talks of losing her nerve. If my favourite writer, Helen Garner, could lose her nerve but keep on going, perhaps I could too. And I did.

So here it is. Seven years after I began it. My essay about writer's block.

About Poetry

There is no perfect time to write poetry, there's only now.
It's time to write poems that rip people's head off,
poems that plunge lives into disarray.

Write them. Write them now. Stanzas so powerful
that the timid finally stand up to their mothers
and say yes to their lovers, verses so tender
that the angry weep
and the grumpy pick lilies for their neighbours.

Get to it. The world needs your inky offerings.
Write poems, poems so bold
that wankers sell their flash houses
and bugger off to the coast,
poems that conjure up ovens,
not in the manner of Sylvia Plath
but in the manner of long slow afternoons
baking pizzas for friends,
oily with herbs and love.

Do it now. Shake the words out of their boxes:
typhoon, marmalade, hippopotamus,
radiant blue miracle, hydrangea, eclipse.

Let the words sing and dance and play
Do it now. Do it now. Do it now.

Certain Difficulties

Virginia Woolf wrote standing up.
So did Hemingway.
Edith Sitwell lay in a coffin.
George Sand made love first.
Colette picked the fleas off her cat and then began.
Schiller sniffed rotten apples.
D. H. Lawrence climbed naked in his mulberry tree.

Others smoked cigars,
took opium,
or wrote while soaking
in the bath.

Kurt Vonnegut tied himself to a chair.

Seems like no one finds
this writing business easy.

Being a Poet

It would be easier not to be a poet.
It would be a fine thing
to come home
watch telly,
untroubled,
mind blank like paper
without need for ink.
Much simpler not to have
a head so full of words
your brain hurts.
It would be good
to see a guy in a beanie
and not feel obliged
to find a metaphor for him.
No need to record,
transform, or consider.
Just be, in the world,
dumb and simple
like a badger or an owl
neither of which I've ever seen
but have read about
in poems.

Fragment

Bring along an exquisite fragment. Bring along two assignments fresh and crisp and ready to mark. Bring along an aching arm. Bring along a squashed salad sandwich in a plastic bag. Bring along a plump, juicy nectarine. Bring a sliver of autumn day, warm around the edge. Bring along the thought of hurrying home to take a boy to basketball practice. Bring along a birthday wish. Bring along a herbal tea bag. Bring along a good idea about what to have for dinner. Bring along the half-written poem sliding around your head. Bring along a hankie just in case. Bring along the memory of a long, sweet night. Bring along two pens in case one runs out. Bring along the subterranean quality of anxiety. Bring one deep breath. Bring along a library card, two dollars sixty-four, a notebook, a giraffe. Bring along a photograph of a long-lost relative. Bring along anything you can't live without. Bring an umbrella, a suitcase, three chocolate frogs. Bring champagne. A postcard. A spare pair of underwear. Bring a half-forgotten secret. An abandoned railway station. Bring along a calendar of the year you were born. A ruby. A night sky. A blade of sweet grass.

Writing in America

I'm on a writing residency in upstate New York, at Ledig House, near Hudson. The buildings are set in a sculpture park. It's nearly fall, and the leaves are beginning to turn. I see deer, groundhogs, squirrels, chipmunks and a fox. At night, wolves howl and the full moon rises over the Catskills

The staff are friendly. My room is quiet. The central heating is a mystery.

The first dinner is prepared by a young Thai chef wearing a jaunty headscarf, who trained in a Chinese restaurant in Bangkok. I'd like to know more about her but she's juggling large pans in a very small kitchen. Prawns in spicy broth, brown rice, fat little mushrooms with fragrant sauce, a platter of broccoli, asparagus and snow peas artfully arranged, pale green melon balls in snowy sago soup.

Writers arrive, each one jet-lagged and anxious about their internet connections. There are many glitches. Then comes a storm. Now we can phone out but no one can phone in. God is messing with us.

On the second night, the Swiss-German is dismissive of me one too many times. I stand in the doorway and say, 'I'm a long way from home. I would like you be nicer to me.' He looks appalled. I hide in my room, feeling ridiculous. The Brazilian comforts me, saying he's like that because he was raised in a small room with bad wallpaper and repressed parents. We laugh. Sao Paulo has thirty million people, she tells me. Don't worry about anythings.

I return to the group. I apologise. They're drinking red wine. I'm wearing my pyjamas. The Swiss-German and I dance to Tom Waits. Around midnight the Chinese writer appears. No one's warned us of her arrival. I mistake her for the Thai chef, though I do wonder why she's standing in the doorway at midnight looking confused.

The charming gay Italian says I remind him of his friend, a British novelist, who is also a witty middle-aged woman. So this is how I am perceived. On Google I find it's true, we resemble each other. An interviewer asks what she has by her bedside, she mentions a basket of postcards to send friends, and a pin to pick her teeth with.

The Chinese writer is very famous, she wrote *Shanghai Baby*. At dinner she speaks vivaciously about astrology, face creams, agents, advances.

The young Spanish writer likes Canadian beer. He's won many prizes and currently holds a scholarship at Princeton. One day he'll be a professor of Spanish Literature but right now they make him teach his language to high-school students. He reminds me of my son. I doubt if I remind him of his mother, unless she's a witty middle-aged writer with odd stuff on her bedside table.

The Swiss-German won't read us any of his own poetry but one night he plays a recording of the great Joseph

Brodsky, then picks up a book that's lying around and reads an Auden poem with great verve.

On the third day the phone lines go down, so does the internet. On the fourth and fifth days it rains continually.

Certain famous people won't take their turn at setting the table or unloading the dishwasher. I want to go home. So this is cabin fever.

The beautiful Slovenian is an actress and a playwright. She says she's been divorced with her husband three times. 'But we have never married.' I realise she means separated. English, you are a fickle, foolish language.

The Russian poet was once an ice skater with a travelling troupe. She has hair like a lion, and a very brown belly because she just spent two weeks in Tunisia. She doesn't say much but gathers squelchy dark-yellow field mushrooms, and fries them with onions, potato and paprika. Despite a frisson of shared anxiety, nobody dies.

The Europeans ask for goats cheese, salami, olives. I want marmalade. I've given up on decent tea. We hang around the kitchen, eating mangoes, blueberries, organic blue corn tortilla chips, bagels, doughnuts. Then we go for long walks, for exercise and inspiration.

A German publisher, Wolfgang, visits. We talk of Munich. I have a fleeting moment of feeling cosmopolitan. However I must stop hoarding peaches and chocolate biscotti in my room, as it is attracting ants.

The Slovenian isn't eating today. She sunbathes by the pool but won't swim because of little frogs and salamanders in the water. Her toenails match her towel. She has very elegant feet.

On Saturday night Wolfgang's friends come to dinner, bringing their old black labrador. The man is Peter Mayer, who ran Penguin for twenty years, and the woman, with whom I talk about tofu and teenagers, is Judith Thurman, *New Yorker* critic and staff writer, author of *Secrets of the Flesh: A Life of Colette*, and *Isak Dinesen: The Life of a Storyteller*.

I am extremely impressed, and set to work on another chapter.

The Finn arrives, fresh from Helsinki. Now it's his turn for dislocation and jet lag. Nice guy. Seems keen to learn about the dishwasher. A boisterous Australian turns up and we call each other 'mate' a lot, because we can't skip between English, Spanish and Russian like the vibrant Tex-Mex girl and the Russian poet.

Sunday. A deer eats apples outside my window. The Italian falls asleep in the lounge, the Swiss-German smokes Camels by the pool, the Brazilian is bored, the Slovenian is homesick, and I feel cosmopolitan all day long.

A Day in the Life of a Writer

8am. Wake up. Look out window. Check weather. Weather is important. Drink a glass of hot water with lemon. Health and bowels are important. Meditate for half an hour. Calmness is important. Make breakfast tray. Pot of strong tea, two slices of wholegrain toast. One with marmalade and thick Greek yoghurt. One with avocado and tomato. Food is very important. Take phone off the hook. Go back to bed. Eat, drink and read for half an hour, or longer. This is called research. Reading matter: cooking magazines, glossy supplements from the weekend paper, poetry books, art books, an old *New Yorker*. Occasionally make a small note about something. Low culture is important. Read horoscope and decide what to cook for dinner. Elizabeth Jolley said she could never start writing for the day until she'd worked out what to have for tea that night.

10am. Have shower, brush teeth, etc. Get dressed in writing outfit: baggy trousers, loosest possible bra, comfy warm top, cosy socks, slippers. Must be comfortable or can't possibly write. Add earrings, to show have not completely turned into a bag lady. Check email. Spend next hour or so doing administrative tasks. This can include googling crossword puzzle answers, sending bio-note to a school or a writers festival, sending a poem to a friend, sensible correspondence with publisher, editor, student.

11am. Take break between business and writing by going for brisk walk. Exercise is important. Let brain roam free and look at things: sky, gardens, cats, passers-by, letterboxes, squashed frog on road. Return to study. Work on book, article, poem, until bored. Make a cup of tea, probably Earl Grey but sometimes jasmine. Return to study, work on whatever I am working on. If writing a novel, goal is five hundred words a day. Good words. The right words in the right order, as Coleridge said, though not to me.

2.30ish. Seek food. Tasty leftovers, if have any. Otherwise soup. Often vegetable, sometimes chicken. Eat lunch, while reading something. Take vitamins: multi, fish oil, St John's wort. (Most writers are melancholy.) Drink green tea, high in antioxidants. Do small tasks such as take scraps to compost, put rubbish out, begin cooking dinner, phone a friend, the lawn mower guy, optometrist. Or, look out the window for a long time, wondering if should have become a documentary filmmaker, or be living in New York, running a funky cafe.

4 o'clock. Research, aka watching a cooking show. Then back into study to work on whatever I am working on. Alternatively, visit library, stationery shop, delicatessen. Perhaps meet a friend for literary gossip, book swapping, discussion about the meaning of life. Also known as research. Think a bit. Do sensible errands. More drinking of tea. Caffeine is most important.

After a day of working, cook dinner, chopping carrots and sprinkling spices, glad to get out of my head and into my body. After eating, watch telly, but only if it is intelligent, or funny. Preferably both. If nothing on telly, read. Often end up writing a list or two. This can make life seem ordered rather than chaotic. Write in journal. Check email. Look at the moon, languish in a hot bath, turn off the light at midnight.

Sometimes I do other stuff, such as edit for money, teach creative writing, plan my teaching, travel, give a radio interview, write a book review or an article, attend a book launch, surf the net, listen to the radio, go to a movie, visit an art gallery. I like to hang out with creative people. I also enjoy asking questions, of the man in the delicatessen, the woman on the bus, or the kid at the skateboard park. You can get away with it when you say you're a writer. I aim to balance thinking and doing, intimacy and solitude, pleasure and pain, hard work and lazy bits. My bank balance is reasonable, although my income arrives in fits and starts. I can sleep in, stay in my pyjamas all day, travel the world and claim it on my tax. So there you have it, the writer's life.

On Writers Festivals

I've been an invited guest at quite a few, including the Adelaide, Melbourne and Brisbane Writers Festivals, in my years as a writer. It's a very odd life.

You're put up in an extremely posh hotel. Your publisher pays for your broadband and your room service. (No wonder publishers are going broke.) After that, you're on your own.

One year, before I knew the above, I lived on bread and cheese and mandarins, bought with my own money, until I learnt I could order room service. When I asked my publicist how come, she told me that they didn't actually tell writers about it because they tended to go silly regarding the mini-bar.

It's often a lonely time, with a handful of intensely social interactions. You walk an unfamiliar town in the afternoon, drifting like a leaf, then at night frock up and talk talk talk, pretending to be intelligent, witty, well-known and fabulous.

The best moment I ever had at a WF was when Helen Garner chatted to me under a tree, and admired the vintage floral dress I was wearing. The worst moment was being seated beside Shaun Tan at a book signing table. Shaun signed copies of his masterpiece, *The Arrival*, for over an hour while I sat quietly beside him, trying not to die of mortification. I signed six books, as I remember, and a cardboard fork for a kid who had no idea who I was. Another disappointment was in Adelaide, at my first major WF. I had a dreadful sinus infection and all I could think of during the swish party thrown by Penguin, abundant with good champagne and handsome young men, was that I needed to go back to my hotel and lie down.

There's always a green room at writers festivals, where the writers and publicists hang out, waiting for their moment in the sun. There's usually an urn in which the water is lukewarm. I drink tea, so this is a sorrow. You'll have to ask someone else about the coffee situation. I hear it's not very favourable. Sometimes there are staleish cakes and pastries, at best, an ample fruit platter. When lunch arrives, the best sandwiches and panini are quickly taken. By the fifth day, one becomes churlishly sick of bread products, longing for salad, sushi, soup. The crew, in their funky t-shirts with WF logo, hand out bags and information packs, and ignore the urn. Important people are glued to their phones, the rest of us make small talk, except the truly introverted, who ping away at their laptops or hide behind the free newspapers. A common topic, even for the very famous, is the lack of publicity given to their book. In Brisbane I hung around with the fairly famous. Michael Morpurgo borrowed an emery board from me, and Mary-Anne Fahey showed me a weird wiggly thing she used to do with her little toe to freak her sister out.

Most writers are shy. Les Murray, Australia's best-known poet, is very shy but Elizabeth Honey is an exception. She's extroverted and friendly, and has very red hair and a very green outfit. She's a bit like New Zealand's Margaret Mahy, except younger. She was indeed a honey, and invited me to have dinner with her German collaborator and some other classy people, but I was too shy to go.

Sometimes heaps of people come to your gig and you feel world-class and world-famous. My audience are teenagers, with a handful of librarians, teachers, and want-to-be-writers. I have only one presentation, which involves telling the story of how I came to be a writer, how I work, how the industry is structured, how much money I make, strung together with literary anecdotes and a joke or two. When I run out of steam I ask for questions and give long intricate answers, until my forty minutes are up. Usually my presentation goes down really well; occasionally it falls flat. C'est la vie. Regarding the audience size, sometimes there's a large marquee or full auditorium. Occasionally there are only seven people, all of whom look bored. On those days one reminds oneself of the flash hotel and the fat cheque, which are yours regardless of the size of the audience and their adoration of you or lack thereof. There are other benefits, if one can ignore one's wounded pride and focus on them. For a writer, it's a chance to mix with peers, to get a sense of one's readers, to experience the life and times of another city, and wear real clothes for a change.

The highlight of Brisbane for me was the opening night cocktail party, complete with ice sculpture, soft jazz, elegant food. Everyone was dressed to the nines. Champagne in hand, the writers stood together on the patio. It was tropical, it was fabulous. We were part of something big and buzzy, something grand. The others went to dinner, but I was replete after the wonderful canapés. I strolled back to the hotel along the palm-lined river, pampered and elegant. Another night I ventured to the Pumphouse, to hear a late session of Armistead Maupin and Patrick Gale indulging in literary gossip. Great fun.

People often ask if writers festivals are worth attending. I think they are. It's a chance to listen to the best writers, to buy books, to be exposed to new ideas, to widen your literary horizons. It's a smorgasbord. You won't like everything at the table, but if you are lucky you'll find plenty to eat, and much of it will be tasty.

Lost Poetry

I lost poetry somewhere along the way. I was too busy doing the dishes and trying to please everyone. I washed a thousand nappies, baked healthy cakes, returned all phone calls. I burned up all my energy on sensible things. Somehow I managed to buy my Christmas gifts in plenty of time each year. Me, a Buddhist, with no real feeling for that chubby man in a red suit with his white beard and his team of mad-eyed reindeer! I even made my own greeting cards. People liked my dinner parties. Being alive was a full-time job for me.

I wasn't happy but I was functioning. I could hold up my end of a conversation, but I always had one eye on the door.

Poetry got lost. Oh, there were books on my shelf. Sexton, Heaney, Plath. But the real poetry was no longer in me.

I also forgot to dance. I was too busy writing lists, and doing the things on them.

One Thursday afternoon in the early autumn of my life, although it was spring in real time, I looked in the mirror.

There she was. A solemn creature, with no hint of poetry about her.

It was a sad moment, for a life without poetry is a slow death.

I set off in search of poetry, for poetry is always there when one goes looking.

I began in my garden, amongst the bright nasturtiums, wearing a blue satin kimono. One must be suitably attired, for poetry is reluctant to visit the unimaginative dresser. It is important to embroider the edges of your life with chrysanthemums.

When forced by circumstances beyond my control to shop at a large supermarket, I danced the rumba in the car park, but I learned that poetry has, for the most part, deserted shopping malls and can more easily be found in small Italian shops, shining among the eggplants.

Never again will I tell myself that I have fucked up my whole life, for this is cruel and there is no poetry to be found in cruelty. Even though I am a dark-haired woman of a certain age who was once beautiful but who now has a wrinkly neck, I must remember that I come from a long line of gypsies and that it is possible for me to live happily in a world changing so rapidly that even a loaf of bread has a website.

I hold fast to my opinion, which is that a loaf of bread has no need for a website. All a loaf of bread needs is a good crust, a bit of chew, and to have been baked with love.

So, dear friends, gathered here tonight in various stages

of elegance and disarray, let us go forth into our lives and fill them full of poetry. Let us go beyond the bounds of normalcy, dancing wildly, leaping like mad things into the creative beyond. Let us forget what we have been told to do, and do the things we love to do for life is short and art is big and life is made for living.

Things that are hard to say

OCCASIONS WHEN TIME DRAGS BY

Things that make the heart lurch with anxiety

THINGS WHOSE OUTCOME YOU LONG TO KNOW

ON memoir

My Inky Life: Thoughts About Writing Memoir

> *Shall I tell the truth? Line up all the facts, as tidy as a row of pins? No, for the truth is just a wire you walk along, stepping gingerly until you meet thin air, and facts are stale old things, wrinkled as dried mushrooms. Why not plump them out a little, soak them until they swell, rearrange the aunties and make my boyfriends even more handsome than they were. We were a family of odd bods and every summer we spent by the river. At night the morepokes called again and again.*

Not everyone wants to write autobiographical material. Some stories are best crafted as fiction, and there are some matters that are too hard to write about. Sometimes it is best to let our stories go to ground, perhaps for years, before bringing them into the light. Writing about family can be shark-infested water, because we may have mixed feelings about our kin. Family is a site of pleasure and pain, memory and desire, fire and tears, story and ink and wine and blood. As Ashleigh Brilliant said, 'If you don't believe in ghosts, you've never been to a family reunion.'

Writing about our life can help untangle the turmoil of the past. As Jeanette Winterson wrote, 'If you tell yourself like a story, it doesn't seem so bad.' Or in the words of Audre Lorde, 'I wrote to save my own life.'

But memoir must be more than struggle laid bare on the page. Insight is required, not mere self-indulgence. It helps to have a clear aim for your work. When planning 'The Queen of Everything Soup' I wrote, 'I'd like this book to address things that matter to me. I am interested in food, Buddhism, depression and healing, social justice, creativity, death, technology, travels small and large.' When I lost my way, I returned to my initial vision as a reminder. Anne Lamott, author of *Bird by Bird*, says it better. 'I try to write the books I would love to come upon, that are honest, concerned with real lives, human hearts, spiritual transformation, families, secrets, wonder, craziness – and that can make me laugh. When I am reading a book like this, I feel rich and profoundly relieved to be in the presence of someone who will share the truth with me, and throw the lights on a little'. This, I think, is what the best memoir does. It shares the truth and throws the lights on a little.

Memoir is a rich, ever-changing genre. If you want to write memoir, read widely, exploring and investigating the field, and eventually go beyond that, finding your own voice, diving deep into your own imagination, into the blood and guts and breath of your life. There are questions worth considering. What are you prepared to share in the public sphere and what might best remain private? Is this story yours to tell? Avoid betrayal, appropriation and revenge; they will leave a very sour trace. How can you stretch the possibilities of language? How might you use landscape, time, white space, to craft your material? What details will give authenticity? What will surprise, delight, horrify or intrigue your reader, making your work shine?

Beth Kephart's *Handling the Truth: On the Writing of Memoir* is one of the best books I've read on the subject. Kephart is passionate about the subject and her writing is poetic, sane, inspiring. She's won many awards and teaches at Penn University. 'Be awake to the world,' she tells her students. Her book is a delight to read and if her writing exercises don't get you writing, you are probably a lost cause. *Thinking About Memoir,* by Abigail Thomas, is another excellent resource. Her own book, *A Three Dog Life,* about her husband's accident and ensuing brain damage, is one of the finest I've read. In *Thinking About Memoir* she writes, 'Keep your eyes and ears open, also your heart. Be Honest. Dig Deep. Or don't bother.' This calls to mind what Anne Michaels replied when asked why it took eight years to write *Fugitive Pieces*: 'Because every time I thought I was getting shallow, I stopped.' Extraordinary integrity is called for when writing memoir. You will have to dig into the dark true places, and write them beautifully. The reader will know if you did not say true things, or hurried towards the end, and you will know it too. The jewels may be buried. Take your time.

The door is a mouth, a sound, a word. There are windows of light and the odd porthole. A carpet of old poems. A kitchen cluttered with brightly coloured cups, plates, and adjectives. On the desk are a pile of neatly arranged ideas, and a vase of freesias interspersed with thoughts and delicate green ferns. In the bedroom there is a pair of velvet slippers embroidered with lies. Here in the place of the drunken heart and the snowflake ball.

When I was ten, my father killed himself. My mother died of Korsakoff's syndrome, an alcohol-related disease, when I was twenty-two. My oldest sister died of a brain tumour. Her first child had died of leukaemia aged two. These deaths affected me deeply. It's no surprise that in my teenage novels, although it was never a conscious decision, you'll find dead fathers, absent fathers, crazy fathers, loving mothers, nutty mothers, and a host of young adults struggling with the idea of family. It is also unsurprising that I provided my readers with happy endings. We can't control what happens in the big world but in fiction we can make the puppets dance any way we like. Both readers and writers find solace in stories where things can turn out just right, because in life sometimes they don't.

Memoir is a different kettle of fish. In memoir, events are not under our control, although the way we choose to tell them is. Memoir takes us into gritty territory, into the hard places. The novel I wrote for my master's degree, now destined to live in a drawer forever, was messy and chaotic, like the life that spawned it. It was a mixture of brilliant bits and shabby bits, a full-length work with themes of death, trauma, addiction, mental illness and alcoholism. My family provided the raw material but I didn't understand how to structure my material and I didn't trust my own voice enough to write it as memoir.

Instead, I wrote poetry that was autobiographical. The story of my lost father can never fully be told, yet I've often attempted it. *I want to say father, father, into the silence of the past* ... but my words fizzle away, just like his suicide note. I pour my longing, anger and grief onto the page, but it's too late, he's long gone, he can't hear me now.

FATHER'S DAY 1996

I want to put it all in the past
but it won't go.

The Leibovitz photograph.
Mick's suicide wrist –
  tight shrivelled stitches
    tiny black worms burrowing
      in the pallid flesh.

Somewhere behind me
a young woman in front of a mirror
cuts deep with a thin rusted blade
watches the blood dripping down
on her furry slippers
gets sent home from casualty
by a tired intern
does not speak for a year

II
Perhaps I should have done it the way you showed me,
properly, with pills and a note.

Perhaps I should stop
trying to write you a poem.

Carve an epitaph instead.

To my beloved father –
Rest in peace, you bastard.

III
Who are they for,
Spring's wild freesias
blooming on the ragged hill?

My mother's death was sadder and slower. One day, on the phone, she casually complained about problems with her vision. A year later she was dead. Korsakoff's syndrome leaches thiamine from the brain, and my mother's illness was swift, tragic and dreadful. She lost her fierce intelligence, she lost her ability to walk unaided, she no longer recognised family and friends. I stole flowers for her as I walked to the hospital where she lay unconscious. I sang to her, holding her lifeless hand. I was young. I was adrift. In the years that followed I wrote about my mother as a way of bringing her to life, my long-gone mother who should have been a poet but instead took on a man and a bottle and a complex life of bright and shadow that didn't end well.

MOTHER'S DAY 1992

I forgot to wear
a white flower
for my mother
who died so long ago.
This poem instead,
for Irene,
who never went near
a fluffy slipper.

Our lives find their way into our writing, sometimes consciously, sometimes not. It has been said that anyone who's survived childhood has already accumulated a lifetime's worth of material. Are our stories of self real? Well, yes, no, and maybe. Jerome Bruner said that the self is 'a perpetually rewritten story' and Humphrey Carpenter suggests that 'autobiography is probably the most respectable form of lying.' Memoir is a slippery beast, a fluid genre where the self represents the self, where we exaggerate and elaborate our own existence, and memory is a very fluid zone. The facts are already bent; our version of truth has been filtered through culture, desire, language, and the cracked mirror of time. A memoir is one account, a version of things, inhabiting the fertile space between 'reality' and fiction. One could argue that even the notion of self is a construct without stable substance, and that the world itself is fictive, nothing but a wild and wonderful arising and passing away of continually shifting phenomena. We are human and our stories matter so, despite the contentious nature of truth, if the reader comes with us willingly and finds their own meaning in our narrative, surely that is enough.

*

In the park today, I pass a group of children making fishing rods from string and sticks.

'My grandfather ...' a chubby girl begins but no one's listening. She tries again.

'Six months ago my grandfather had a heart attack and died.'

The other kids don't respond; they're engrossed in their task. I want to tell her I'm sorry to hear it but I'm a passing stranger and I don't want to freak her out so I keep walking. Perhaps she didn't require a response. She just needed to say it out loud. Maybe that is why we write memoir. We need to say it out loud.

The Mirrored Surface

I know what they think. I know what they see when they look at me. I see that reflection myself when I walk through elegant department stores, in a rectangular mirror near the overpriced chinaware, and again and again in the lingerie department, walking fast past the French silk nightgowns that no one can afford. Housewife. Ordinary. Getting older, not quite middle-aged, and far from seventeen. The haircut is not stylish enough; when you pay ten dollars for a haircut all you get is a ten-dollar haircut. This ordinary woman in black sweat pants and a nowhere sort of jumper. Cheap earrings, fake diamonds. Legs and bum too large. A serious face, pale with the long winter and wrinkled from too many summers. Once upon a time when sitting in the sun was healthy ... Ah, but here and now she carries a plastic bag containing a wholemeal sandwich loaf and a cauliflower, to make some soup for dinner. An ordinary woman. This is all you can see.

It is not all there is. There is more but they only see the ordinariness, the thin veneer. There is more, there is more, there is more.

In my writing class we fill the idle moments with close surveillance of each other. We stealthily watch and judge, meticulous and cruel. Harry's nose is stretched with conceit and I am happy that dazed, soft Miriam ignores his calculated attempts to impress her. I spend a lot of time watching. I like to watch fat Rose. I admire her. She brings her junk food every day and has no shame, eating it, eating, always eating. Her podgy face has a kindness and she always says hello, not like Harry, who pretends I don't exist, because I am beneath him. Ah, yes, I know them so well, these people, inside my head. In truth I do not know them well at all, and they know nothing of me. I know that they watch me as I watch them, and have me labelled and neatly arranged in the Madame Tussaud galleries behind their eyes. They see old. Straight. Probably married to a public servant, two kids, boring names – Anne and Simon? Shouldn't wear that striped thing, it makes her look bigger. Always gets her work in on time, drinks tea, lives in a brick and tile in a tidy suburb, or a duplex ...

It is of no consequence but I want to tell them all about me, all that I have done, about what lies beneath the mirrored surface. I want them to know that I was born on a floral carpet with jazz playing, and a bunch of freesias in a jar nearby. I want them to know that my mother was a gypsy queen and that I slept on an old bit of satin in a leather suitcase until I grew too big. I want to tell them that my father collected Hawaiian shirts and women, and died by his own hand. Can't they see that I've tried more drugs than they have ever heard of, and sold good grass to the chief of police in Papeete, way back in '72 ... smoked with him on the beach and fucked him like crazy all night long under a palm tree, and went and ate croissants at the Tahiti Hilton, and fell asleep. These kids should know that I have had more lovers than surprises and that I have very few regrets.

One day when the tutor is going on about metaphors, I will shout 'Hey!' and throw my shoes out the window and tell them all the funny things I ever did and all about Thailand, and Africa, and what it's like in jail. I think they should know that at their age I had an abortion, and cried for a week, and that Max gave me a bunch of wilting irises, and ran off with my best friend. As part of my fertility saga I could tell them about the waitressing job in the sleazy Indian restaurant and the baby that grew in my belly after I gave in to Chandra's oily insistence and opened my legs for him, surrounded by an audience of dirty curry pots. I was so lonely then. I didn't like Chandra but I grew to love the thought of a baby with long dark eyelashes swimming happily inside me, like in the pictures in the pregnancy books from the library. About three months down the line I awoke to hot blood all over my nightgown and that was the death of those hopes and dreams. I cried like hell, and I carried on. That's what you have to do. I might add that Sydney was a hard town with a mean edge, and that when they found Mercedes three days dead, with 'Fuck You All' written on her mirror in lipstick it was time to move on. After the funeral they gave Claudia her sister's ashes in a pizza box and we drank gin and threw the ashes into the air under the magnolia trees in the botanical gardens, and I left town, and Claudia went back onto smack.

I have thirty-seven years crammed with stories. Which stories would they like the most? Somehow it seems that sex is a preoccupation of youth, so I could speak of seducing

Lily under the jasmine bush and all those months of breast and cunt and sweetness, until she got the scholarship and went away. I might mention to the handsome boy who sits at the back of the room and whose face is so charming and open that his firm body in my bed sounds like a good idea to me, if he's ever round my way. I'd like them all to know that I make real bread, hot and plaited, and pasta dripping with oily mushrooms and capsicums and tomatoes and that I always buy the very best sharp parmesan to grate over the top. That I lived in the country and survived a flood and a fire, but not a marriage. That I had a proper breakdown, and spent a year in silence, and never can remember how to play chess. That I bring my son up as best I can, and that I think that having a kid is the hardest job of all, and that I don't recommend it unless they are damn sure. That I've been a waitress and a dealer and a dancer and a teacher and lost some dreams and kept some and hope that all of their dreams come true. I want to tell them that I spent my whole childhood wanting to be ordinary, to get away from my beat-up family with their beat-up lives, and that ordinary is dreary and that special is the best. I wish I could show them my angel statue from Indonesia and the anemones in my pink blue silent evening garden. I want to tell them that my auntie bred snakes and that everything changes, that life can be hard, but you must treat it softly and that love is not solid and that booze does not help.

Tell me your stories, Miriam, Harry, Rose. I'd like to hear them, your bits and pieces, your lies and your truths. Let's travel together, down the long white road of the page.

Good Voodoo – a Short Story

I went to the art gallery today and saw interesting things. A piece of old floral carpet cut into a ragged shape, as if it were the pelt of a large beast. Ed Ruscha's *Exploding Cheese*. It was very quiet in the gallery, hallowed ground somehow, and when I left I looked more kindly on the day and on my circumstances. I ate a bowl of noodles in the food hall, bought mandarins and coloured pencils. So much freedom for me now. No bells, no gongs, no schedule. Just head out the door and start walking. No one to ask or tell. Just go. Just do. I walk for miles, exploring the city of my birth, so foreign to me now but eerily overlaid with the murky memories of a girl with my name, who swam here, fucked there and was lonely all over the place.

I've been many things and now I am none of them. For nine years I was a Buddhist nun. I can't entirely explain why I left the temple, even to myself. You could blame it on the bitter Korean winters. Or my ill health: the constant fatigue from eating rice and pickles and not enough protein. Perhaps it was seeing the families coming to the temple with their beautiful children. I wanted one of those fat Buddha babies. Perhaps it was the dreams I began to have. A dream of a diamond button. A dream of adopting four children, then giving one back. A dream of twigs in the hair. The more twigs you had in your hair the more people liked you. A dream of a dress festooned with blue roses. These dreams of yearning gathered like full dark clouds. It was time to leave, so I left.

The head of my temple was kind. The formalities were simple, the ceremony was short. Often I'd been the one to cook the farewell meal. This time Seijo prepared it. Miso soup with seaweed and mushrooms, sweet rice cakes, green tea. Afterwards the nuns returned to their chores before evening chanting. Suddenly I was afraid. I took a deep breath and walked out onto the noisy street. My jeans felt stiff and my sneakers were a bit too big. Everything was bright and loud. On the plane my neighbour drank whiskey then fell asleep slumped against my shoulder. My skin had not touched the skin of a man in nine years.

So, here I am, back in Auckland. I ring my parents to say I'll be down to see them soon. I don't call my sister. No one visits, except a few midnight mosquitoes. I am older than I want to be, more anxious. I can't seem to live the wisdom I have studied for so long. Over and over I forget the simple truths: to live simply, to desire nothing, to accept what arises and be happy.

Reading the paper freaks me out. So much suffering in the world: famine, corruption, murdered children. I entered the temple to learn to be at peace with suffering but here's the thing. I am not at peace with it. The buskers on Queen Street freak me out as well, especially the eerie man with an artificial arm who stands motionless on a box.

His handwritten sign says 'Move for silver, sing for gold, smile for free', but everyone just hurries past. There's a stoned kid with angry eyes crouched in a doorway, and down near the Ferry Building a huge man with pee stains on his trousers rattles a Starbucks cup containing a few small coins. I don't feel compassion. I feel pity mixed with disgust, for myself as much as for them. I'm selfish. I want joyous buskers. I want naked midgets throwing confetti, a wistful Irish beauty playing the violin. I want swarthy twins performing magic tricks, like in an elegant movie. Everyone on the street looks distracted. They're wired for sound or busily texting as they walk. I don't belong in the modern world. I want to be back in Korea, except I didn't want that when I had it, either.

Each day I walk and walk, remembering things: the deep green of the harbour, the taste of smoked fish. I marvel at what's sprung up since I left: sushi bars, Pacifica shops, the Sky Tower glowing electric in the night.

When I'm not walking, I sit in the afternoon sun, drinking green tea and writing lists. Devonport. Library. Spices? It feels strange to have hair. I stroke my head when I'm alone. It feels good, soft like moss, short like a lawn.

I've been putting off seeing my sister. When we were children we were friends: two wild girls with dark plaits, playing hula hoops and climbing trees. Joyous. By the time we were teenagers Marla and I were competing for everything: our parent's approval, our grandmother's money. Then we stopped fighting and just avoided each other. Marla thought my meditation retreats were crap. I despised her expensive tastes and her rich husband, bland as porridge. The day I referred to him as The Ken Doll, Marla threw her shoe at my head.

I can't put it off any longer, so when Marla phones I agree to meet in Ponsonby for lunch. I wear my new op-shop outfit: black skirt, black silk shirt, black pumps. I look okay. I walk along Karangahape Road past the anti-nuclear posters, past the park where I dropped acid with my first boyfriend under the dark trees. I'm early so I wait near the door, watching yummy mummies and well-dressed older women come and go. When Marla arrives it takes a moment to recognise her because she's morphed into one of our artistic aunts. She's plumper and a bit worn-looking, but stylishly gaudy in layers of velvet and turquoise suede boots. We hug. She smells of gardenias and her boobs are pleasantly squashy. I'm surprised how glad I am to see her.

'Hey girl.'

'Hey girl, you.'

We are shy. There's a clumsy moment as we both try to let each other enter the cafe first. It's pretty flash, with dark wood, white damask linen and jazz playing softly. There are too many choices on the menu. I panic and order a Greek salad so I won't have to think about it any longer. Marla chooses the seafood omelette which immediately seems a far better option. I'm starting to feel unglued. This place is too fancy for me. I expect small talk but Marla dives straight in.

'Why did you leave?'

'The temple?'

'Well, that too, but I meant why did you leave Auckland?'

'God, Marla. Ask me something easy.'

'No, I want to know. You just took off to Korea. You didn't even say goodbye properly.'

'I did so.'

'You did not.'

I want to remind her of our last phone call, in which she called Buddhism hippy-trippy bullshit, but the waiter arrives and by the time he's delivered some olives and poured our water I've had time to gather myself. Breathe into it, I tell myself. Stay in your body. Marla, however, doesn't seem to be channelling the Dalai Lama. She rips onwards, guilting me about the fact that I didn't come home for our grandmother's funeral. Next she'll start on why I haven't bothered to visit our parents yet.

'Can I borrow your car? I need to go to Palmerston North to see Mum and Dad.' Ha, that fooled her. A brief victorious moment. Suddenly I'm six years old again. I've taken her statue of a white china horse and hidden it under my pillow. I remember the feeling of victory. The horse was mine. The joy was brief. I hopped into bed that night and as I lay down I heard the crunch of tiny china legs breaking.

'Yeah, you can borrow the car. Or I could come with you. We could do a sister road trip.'

I'm surprised but try not to show it.

'That would be good. I was thinking of heading down this weekend though.'

'Okay.'

'Don't you need to check with Gerald? I thought you'd have a huge social plan that needed readjusting.'

'Gerald left me.'

'What? When?'

'Six months ago.'

'Why didn't you tell me?'

'It was such a cliché. My husband took off with his secretary. I couldn't bear to write it down. Didn't they censor your mail there, anyway?'

'No. It was a Buddhist temple, not a weird cult.'

'I wasn't sure if they read your mail. Anyway, it was very uncertain for a couple of months. Gerald was wavering but he finally wavered in her direction.'

'Arsehole,' I say. It came out a bit louder than I meant it to, just as the waiter arrives with my salad.

'Not you,' I tell him.

'Excuse me?'

He can't have heard the arsehole bit. Marla giggles.

'The omelette won't be long,' he says, hurrying away.

'You've bewildered the handsome boy child.'

'Do him good.'

We're both grinning. Finally I really look at my sister. I see her saggy neck. I see her wise blue eyes and her killer smile.

'You know the saddest thing?' asks Marla. 'Now that the dust has settled, I'm glad. Whatever was good between me and Gerald was long gone. I just didn't have the guts to leave. Pitiful really.'

'Sounds like you're being pretty hard on yourself.'

'Yeah, that's what my therapist says.'

'Transitions are bumpy, that's for sure.'

I refrain from saying, 'I told you Gerald was a peanut.'

The omelette arrives and we dig in.

'So, why *did* you leave the temple?'

'I'll tell you in the car,' I say. 'It's a long story. It'll take from the Bombay Hills to Hamilton. Can I try your omelette?'

'Sure.' She plops a big piece on top of my salad. We had a good thing going with eggs when we were kids. Marla liked the yolks, I preferred the whites. Our mother would fry eggs for us, cut them up and serve them accordingly, on buttered toast with a sprig of parsley. I'm about to embark upon foods of our childhood but Marla speaks first.

'He wanted me to get Botox.'

'You're kidding.'

'No. He's thinking of getting Botox as well. He's terrified of looking old.'

'Idiot,' I say. 'Not you,' I tell our waiter, who's topping up our water. He smiles.

'Coffee?'

'Jasmine tea.'

Marla orders a latte.

'Why don't we go today?' she says. 'It's a good day for a road trip.'

'Really?

'Yeah, why the hell not. Let's get our stuff and hit the road. Surprise them. Mum will have kittens. It'll do her good.'

'You're on,' I say.

A homeless guy is fossicking in the rubbish bin outside the cafe. He hauls out a piece of half-eaten pizza and starts eating it.

'Don't stare at me, rich bitches!' he yells.

'Don't yell at us, rubbish bin man!' Marla yells back. 'My

sister's a Buddhist nun. She'll put a voodoo curse on you!'

She cackles like crazy. The man grins and shuffles past. Suddenly I feel foolishly happy. Perhaps this world is big enough to contain everything, including me.

Old Black Telephone

For Bob Lowry (1912–1963)

I will sing you to life. I will sing you to life, Bob Lowry, with your baggy Hawaiian shirt and your reckless smile. I will come into your study full of books and hang around. I will fiddle with the standard lamp, ask for paper, use the black pen. I will love the soft-eared spaniel you looked after for the man who went to India. I will stare at your hairy body, pink and wet as you climb out of the bath. I will help you set the table, carefully carrying the cold corned beef, the butter, the chutney, the brown half-loaf of bread. I will bring you the sharp knife so you can cut some silverbeet. I will eat the strange dish you made from eggs and onions and peas. I will help you throw the dead sheep into the compost heap, and when we walk through the park under the dappled light of the oaks I will bring you acorns to put in your pocket. I will sit in the back of the dinghy and drag my hand through the water as you row against the tide and your face turns red. I will love you as a child does even though you nearly killed me with your drunk driving. I will hide under the table amongst the men's feet and wait outside the pub for you forever.

I ring you on the old black bakelite telephone. You've been dead for forty-five years. I'd still like to talk to you.

The telephone is a classic. It has a heavy dial, slow and ponderous, with real numbers in a circle. It's exactly like the one we had at One Tree Hill, when I was a kid. I found it in the back of a cupboard in the flat where I'm living as writer-in-residence. I was thirty-five when I became a writer, Dad. Before then I was a scribbler of lines in a notebook, a woman who didn't know what she was meant to be doing with what Mary Oliver calls this wild and precious life.

Remember when I was eight, and you made those two poems of mine into a booklet? They were odd little poems, but not dreadful. One was about gypsies and one was about autumn leaves. You printed a hundred copies, I signed each one and we sold them to unsuspecting relatives for two and sixpence. That was the beginning. Something was planted in me then. The extraordinary idea that someone might value my words and ideas. That perhaps writing was a thing one might do.

But girls did not become writers in those days. We did sensible jobs such as nursing, or teaching, or secretarial work, or we got married. So at seventeen I started my working life as a library clerk in the law school at the university. I found it very boring. I was more interested in marijuana and handsome young medical students, which was not a bad combination, actually, for a while. Jobs were easy-come, easy-go, in those days. If you got sick of something, you chucked it in and did something else. I tried waitressing, at which I was crap, then did a stint as a laboratory assistant, growing germ cultures in agar-agar and putting glass jars into a big steamer. Next came a job in John A. Lee's bookshop, selling car manuals. Occasionally I nicked a little money from the till. What was I thinking? I justified it somehow, but it horrifies me, to remember it now. At twenty I was attractive, in a sulky kind of way. Moody though, and prone to the glooms. I was good with kids so Mum suggested I try teaching. Training college was fun, and my first year of teaching began well, but I was taking too many drugs and my fragile self was held together with cobwebs and spit. I was thin, I got thinner. I was talking to God. I was touching the sky. Until I fell. That's the thing. After the up, you go down down down.

Ah, but I wasn't going to dwell in the past.

About ringing you, and writing about it: I don't want to be one of those sad, messed-up women who never get over the death of their father. It's not like that. It's just that it's late, and I'm lonely.

Can you hear me, Dad?

I've been lonely most of my life, if you want the truth, despite many good friendships and two loving husbands. As the years creep on and those I care about are dying, I realise I don't have forever. I want to make the most of my time, to connect. Anyway, I thought I'd call you. Tell you what's up.

So, the present: it's a rainy Sunday, February 24th, to be exact. I'm living right by Albert Park, in the Sargeson flat. You'd like that, for sure, since you knew Frank. It's good money too, this residency, being funded by a law firm. You wouldn't approve of the law firm but you'd approve of the generous stipend.

As for Auckland, you wouldn't believe how it's changed. The skyline is dominated by a tall, thin building, resembling both a minaret and a giant syringe. Everyone grumbled about the Sky Tower at first but now they've become fond. It's iconic, like the Taj Mahal or the Statue of Liberty. What does it represent, I wonder. Capitalism gone mad? Neon greed? Or is it a tribute to joyousness, to glittery fun? A totem to paradox, perhaps, containing all of the above. If I stand on tiptoes I glimpse it, glowing, from my skylight. It's lit with white light tonight, a red tip on the spire. It'll be green on St Patrick's Day, apparently. At other times it's golden, or blue, or red, or all the colours of the rainbow. People in the rest of the country slag off Auckland. JAFAs, they say. It means 'just another fucking Aucklander'. But I like it here. It's a completely different cultural mix these days. There's a huge Asian population, mainly from China and Korea, thousands of Pacific Islanders and lots of feisty Maori. A city with grunt, vibrant and alive. You can still do the good stuff: swim at the Parnell Baths, walk in the Domain, get the ferry to Devonport. The harbour is a joy. It's a great city for sailing, out on the blue tide, past Rangitoto to Waiheke or Kawau Island. There are some shitty things about Auckland though. Traffic jams like you wouldn't believe, and a hell of a lot of homeless people. The city is full of drifters, of the lost and lonely, especially at night.

Even after all this time, there are many who remember you, Dad. You've entered the mythology of this city, your name is a part of its bohemian past. Most people speak fondly of Bob Lowry, of your big heart and your superb typography. Stories float around about the wonderful parties you and Mum held at One Tree Hill. The less charitable mention your hopelessness with money, your messy fall from grace. Amazingly, the building in Airedale Street where you had your last printing press is still standing. It's painted bright blue, and covered in tagging. What's more, it's up for sale. I'd like to buy it, and turn it into a coffee bar that has jazz, and books, and chess, and peasant food. But it's just a wild idea, of which I have many.

I thought I'd tell you a bit about your descendents. Most of us like to garden, cook, read books, and make things. In the main we enjoy talking loudly and eating too much. Most are fond of a drink. For some, addiction is a problem. Others of us have co-dependency and anger management issues. They talk about issues now, Dad. In your day they probably just said fucked-up.

We may be wobbly in certain ways, but we're an interesting bunch. I think you'd be proud. You've bred a line of creative people: writers, artists, an actor, a policy wonk, a tag artist, an architect, a filmmaker, and a granddaughter with an artisan ginger beer company, to name a few. You'd especially love the new generation of babies, your great-grandchildren. Imagine. Such dear little bubbas. I wish you could hold one on your knee.

I miss you, Dad. Father's day is the worst. Other people honour their fathers with a picnic or a family gathering. For me, it's always a shit of a day. I veer between sad, lost and numb. So many layers of sorrow. There have been other deaths since yours. Mum died twelve years after you did, from an alcohol-related disease. Robin subsequently died of a brain tumour. Neither of them were easy deaths. But the rest of us are alive and kicking. We've still got the place at the Wade River, although the scene is very different now. The bottom bach is gone, replaced by a funky two-storey job with a beautiful deck, and the middle bach is now a reconstructed shed. You loved the green Wade river, the peace and quiet. Remember feasting on cockles, Tom Dooley on the old radio, the morepork in the pine trees? We've planted a tree there for you, a pohutukawa, in a shady grove.

I ran away from New Zealand in my twenties. Lived the high life in Sydney for a few years, then changed direction completely and spent seven years living in a Buddhist community in the bush. I got married and had my son. You'd like him a lot. He's a documentary filmmaker, a creative spirit with a kind heart. I've been a good mother, I think, but not the easiest one, given my history. He's had to live with that. Just like I've had to live without you, all these years.

Sometimes I think you did the right thing, bowing out early. To be honest, if I thought it was that easy to step off the wheel of birth and death, I'd probably have checked out long ago myself. But I believe in karma, which means you get reborn and have to face the music all over again. You'd shout me down over that one, no doubt. You didn't think there was any such thing as God. I imagine you'd have similar feelings about Buddhism. We'll just have to agree to disagree about that one, eh? Having a spiritual life isn't such a bad thing, though. I was reading today about the composer Sibelius. Like you, he found it impossible to work or survive without alcohol. If only there was a way out, he wrote in his diary. Without faith of any kind, he descended into hopelessness. You and Sibelius aren't the only ones to feel this way. Life is hard, suffering can be immense. Many seek escape, not always by dying. Drugs, drink, excessive consuming, obsessive exercising, endless television, overeating – so many ways to avoid pain. Human beings can only bear so much reality, as T. S. Eliot said.

This is what you wrote on your suicide note: *Forgive me. I have taken the coward's way out*. Your sad surrender. I always wondered what happened to that note. Is it hidden in some police file, or was it thrown away? I'll probably never find out. A few years ago I met the guy who found your body. He'd been at the party at One Tree Hill that fatal night. He got wasted and crashed there. In the morning he went to see if you wanted a cup of tea. He was only eighteen. What a shocker for him. As for the note, I don't need to see it. It's indelible, written inside me.

I wasn't going to be all bitter and twisted about your suicide. Mainly I'm not. I understand things had become unbearable for you. You did what you had to do.

I became a writer when I was thirty-five. I had such a bad day as a relief teacher in a hard-arse school in Perth that I went back to university and started to write. The stories poured out of me: your suicide, my failed marriage, things that had happened in my life or lives I had encountered. It wasn't therapy, but it proved a creative road to healing. I haven't looked back. Eight books for teenagers, international sales. Combined with teaching creative writing it's been a solid career. And now I'm slowly finding my way back to my early loves: short fiction, poetry and essays. You would have been a writer too, I reckon, if you hadn't been so busy printing, and trying to make a buck. The letters and poems you left behind prove your talent.

I've inherited a lot from you, not just a love of books and language. I'm keen on Hawaiian shirts. My favourite song is 'Mack The Knife'. I'm a firm believer in compost heaps. I like to hang out with artists and writers. I get bored with sensible people, preferring neurotic, interesting people. Sometimes I talk too much and forget to listen properly. I'm impatient and bossy. Sometimes I get in a rage and throw something, though not very often these days. As for your depression? Yes, I inherited that too. It took me years to admit it, and even more years to say it out loud. I'm going okay, though. I take St John's wort and fish oil. I walk a lot. Buddhist teachings have helped me immeasurably. I do meditation, get counselling when I need it. None of this was offered to you. Maybe if it had been, you'd have come through the darkness and stuck around.

Talking to you is taking me back to some hard places. Remember when we walked through Cornwall Park to visit Kirsty? I was nine, and your first grandchild, not yet three years old, was dying of cancer. The sadness was always with us, after that, and before that too. You were a dark river. I am a dark river too.

This is what I want to know, Dad. If you could ring me up on the old black telephone and tell me something, just one thing, what would it be?

The town is quiet tonight and ghostly. There's a cool edge to the city. Summer's nearly gone. Often I become sorrowful in autumn but this year I'm more relaxed, taking things as they come. Learning to be with things just as they are, not wishing them to be any different. Which sounds easy, but is actually a deep practice. Just this. To enjoy this bumpy life that tastes of soup and pears. This time of writing and thinking, of getting to know Auckland again.

Walking down Airedale Street, I can almost smell the ink. I remember playing in the bin of paper offcuts, and the rhythmic sound of the printing press. I remember waiting in the car for you outside the pub, waiting for you to stop drinking and take me home so Mum could yell at you, and we could have dinner.

I'm walking a lot. Just moodling around. Research, I call it. I'm finding ideas all over the place. I went to the Elam library today, and sat there for ages, reading typography and art books. I looked at photographs of the demolition yard in LA where all the broken neon signs go. I discovered an artist who stencils dance floors with icing sugar, in fancy floral patterns. I read David Shrigley, a Glasgow artist with a fine sense of the absurd. He writes strange, wise, funny things in childish printing. Initially his work appears nutty, misshapen and clumsy but it's actually very profound. One of my favourite lines of his goes like this: 'The best things and the worst things all mixed together in a bag.' I wrote it in my journal. This is what writers do. We make notes in journals and leave them to breathe. Later, if we are lucky, some kind of alchemy occurs. The scribblings and jottings take form. Stories and narratives, poems and prayers, finding their way home, when they are meant to.

What else can I tell you? Well, technology has gone apeshit. Computers and mobile phones, the internet and texting. Some of these things seem fantastic and wonderful to me, and some do not, but that, as they say, is another story. Things that were science fiction back then are everyday now. The pace of acceleration is downright scary. We don't worry about the bomb any more. Now we're threatened by terrorism and global warming. They call it climate change but what it means is that we have stuffed up the planet, big-time. Capitalism has gone crazy, man. In a fancy schmancy wine store in Mt Eden they're advertising Louis Roederer champagne for only $390 a bottle, down from $450. One of Matisse's odalisques was recently auctioned at Christies and sold for $33.6 million. *Hanging Heart* by Jeff Koons went for $23.5 million. So the rich bastards continue to rake it in, even though the planet is rife with poverty and starvation. People are still dying in India, Dad. It is a crazy world and I often wish I wasn't a part of it. But I am.

I woke late this morning, and didn't feel like writing, so I took the day off. Whatever that means. I cleaned the flat then went to town. It was one of those days where everything looks a little awry. A good day for a writer. I saw a radiant Brazilian woman with blue toenails, four young Sikhs, three homeless beggars and a partridge in a pear tree. I ate a plate of delicious rich meaty Malaysian food, bought a new black pen, ate an orange in the sun.

About living alone. I've started talking to myself. Not actual conversations, but I yell *Oh Yeah!* every time something good happens, like when I finally found my missing kitchen scissors. They were down the back of the fridge, along with a hell of a lot of dust, and a slice of Vogel's toast which must have been there for weeks yet still looked perfectly okay. Fossilised toast. It would make a good name for a band.

I'm happy here in Auckland. I like the way you can disappear into a city. I like the odd little life I've created here. I buy nectarines late at night, walk home in the dark feeling contemporary and urban. I see friends in sporadic bursts, when I feel like it, not just to be polite. Above my bed I've hung a tiny jade Buddha and a jade teardrop that I found in St Vinnies, to call in the good dreams. I'm enjoying talking to you on the old black telephone.

Here's a joke for you. You always liked a good joke. My Irish grandfather, your father, loved jokes too. He'd say 'Do you want a big piece of bread or a small one?' If you said big, he'd hand you the whole loaf. If you answered small, he'd give you a tiny crumb. So, here's the joke.

You are on a horse galloping at a constant speed. On your right is a sharp drop-off. On your left is an elephant travelling at the same speed as you. Directly in front of you is a galloping kangaroo and your horse is unable to overtake it. Behind you is a lion, running at the same speed as you. What must you do to get out of this highly dangerous situation?

Answer: Get your drunk arse off the merry-go-round.

Which is what you did, in a way.

It's getting late. I'm tired. I offer you the sound of rain.

I've been writing to you all my life, in various ways. I was so angry with you. But I'm not angry with you now. This is for you, Dad. A small offering from a printer's daughter with ink in her veins.

Dear Pat

For my stepfather, Patrick Dobbie (1913–1998)

Dear Pat, I worry about what will happen to your stuff when you die. I don't suppose it really matters. You'll be gone and your things will have outlived their function. Your daughters will have their work cut out for them. No doubt they will do what has to be done. They are capable women, as I remember. Your house is old and your garden has gone crazy. Grapefruit and oranges rot beneath the trees. There are guavas and feijoas and huge clumps of lilies; the jasmine has taken over what's left of the shed. You counted the number of oranges one year, some extraordinary amount. Another year you made a small mark each time you climbed the stairs to your workshop, and on New Year's Eve you added up all the clumps of ten and made a note of it on the back of an envelope. You tally things that no one else would bother with, having a mind that likes exactness. Which would have come in handy in all your jobs. You have been a ballet dancer, a watchmaker, a milkman, an aeronautical engineer, a radio announcer, and a printer – and each of those things need precision in their various ways. You're the only person around who has the patience and the engineering ability to fix the print heads on daisy wheel printers or certain older style jukeboxes. Fewer and fewer jobs come your way now, in these days of the slick and the disposable, but you take great pride in doing things for friends, like fixing a toaster or making a wooden rack for plates.

Pat, your house and the way things are there are totally unique. You have kept every yoghurt pot, every tobacco packet and every old magazine that you have ever had. They are neatly stacked right up to the ceiling in what was once the laundry. You wash your clothes in the bathtub after your weekly bath which you heat with a giant immersion heater that you've rigged up. You don't have the hot water on, for that would be wasteful. Your attic is full of offcuts of paper and cardboard from the printing press days, to the delight of the boldest of the neighbourhood kids who visit you for bundles to draw pictures on. Your printing presses are still there, and the lathes, and a guillotine machine, and all the small pieces of watchmaking gear, in the tiny drawers of beautiful old boxes. Everything is dusty. The bookshelves are full of faded, leather-bound novels and mouldy textbooks. In the glass-covered cupboard are treasures I wanted for my own: shells and snowflake ornaments and bright tin toys. Bits of people's lives are everywhere, paintings and boxes of stale clothing and calendars and photographs and suitcases and the remains of a rocking horse.

You were a forerunner of the conservation movement, the original greenie. You have always been ideologically sound. Who else would take the cream from half a dozen bottles of milk and put it in a jar, then rig up an old washing machine to gently shake the jar back and forth until butter had been made? Or make alfalfa sprouts by the light of one watt inside an old defunct fridge, or buy bags of chicken skin for soup? For years you made yoghurt from a rubbery plant that needed rinsing each week, thick pungent yoghurt as substantial as sour cream. You gave me some of the plant once but mine never came out right so eventually I chucked the rubbery matter away.

Last time I visited I brought a fruitcake and a pot plant and a set of thermal underwear which you liked very much. My son pottered in the depths of the garden while we hacked into the cake and drank strong tea from the pot with the grubby woollen cosy. Your bad leg was stretched on the chair in front of you and I perched on the rickety cane one trying to look comfortable while you told me about the electricity inspector's visit. This bloke was doing a routine visit but your situation was far from routine. There was the giant immersion heater for one thing, plus an extravaganza of self-rigged wiring connecting the downstairs radio to a decent speaker in the upstairs workshop, and your reel-to-reel tape deck was delicately wired to goodness knows what. I think there was some kind of doorbell-cum-alarm system too, and a kettle hooked up beside your bed so you could make tea when hip pain woke you in the night.

The electricity chap had never seen such a Heath Robinson arrangement or so many double plugs in all his life. He phoned his superior, who came to have a look, and he called someone else. You ended up with half a dozen of these jokers following wires into walls and out again, tut-tutting about the possibility of being burnt to death. 'Preferable to a rest home,' you muttered, but in the end you phoned an old electrician friend who agreed to tidy it up to the Electricity Department's specifications and only charge you a minimal amount, for old time's sake.

We were drinking our third cup of tea when you told me about the two social workers who turned up on your doorstep around the same time. They came out of the blue as far as you were concerned but maybe a well-intentioned neighbour had brought them onto the scene. Who knows the mysterious workings of the universe? Perhaps the Electricity Department dobbed you in. The social workers, a man and a woman, were young, still wet behind the ears, you told me indignantly. Your first reaction was to not let them in, but certain courtesies had be adhered to if you wanted the right sort of report to be filed. So you rinsed off your most presentable cups, made a pot of tea and listened as they wriggled on their chairs and suggested that a retirement village would be clean, comfortable and suitable for you in your remaining years. You did not agree and told them so, politely but firmly. The man became bolder, less circumspect.

'It's chaotic. I couldn't live here,' he blurted.

Even now I can hear you replying as you began to show them to the door in such a way as to give them no choice but to leave. You used your best radio announcer's voice.

'Relax, young man. No one has invited you to live here, and I don't intend to do so. Good afternoon.'

God knows what they wrote in the report, but they never came back. A small but important victory, that one. Dear Pat.

I could ring you up right now, but you're nearly deaf, so our words knock into themselves as we fumble with our love and affection across the miles. I only do it on your birthday and at Christmas, when such feelings can't be ignored. There you still are. At this time of year the trees will still be abundant with the oranges that my mother used to make into marmalade. We ate it on thick brown bread topped off with your splendid yoghurt. Listening to the radio together, the three of us, all those musty years ago. What are you doing right now? Are you pottering around up in the workshop, or rolling a cigarette, with your leg resting on the chair? Perhaps you're playing Vivaldi, or reading a book someone has brought you, or drifting off to sleep on your bed by the French doors that lead out into the garden.

Sisters

We are sisters. We are born on the side of a green hill. We run wild. We yell and scream. We hide in cupboards and spy on people. We help our father dig up new potatoes. He wears his Hawaiian shirt and sings 'Goodnight Irene' and 'The Red Flag'. We climb trees. We tell lies. We chase sheep in the park then run home madly. We go to the library and get out books. Our mother is in the Good Food League. She feeds us carrot sticks, brown bread and freshly squeezed grapefruit juice but she drinks sherry. We are sisters. We run wild on the slopes of a green hill. Pink tea roses climb in the window of the wooden house and purple wisteria drapes over the garden wall. We are the four daughters of Robert William and Irene Ethel but we are not given middle names so we make them up. Robin becomes Robin Pansy Primrose Violet Lowry. Judith adds Lucy. Brigid takes a fancy to Gloria while Vanya's pseudonyms are Aurelia Atom Bomb and Bohemia Cutaway. At party time we grate wax on the wooden dance floor and pull each other round on sacks. It is as smooth as glass. *Oh the shark, babe, has such teeth, babe, but he keeps them out of sight.* At dinnertime we sit together on an old sofa while our father rages at the kitchen table. There is stew all over the wall and a plate flies out the window. We hide our faces and our feelings. We go to Epsom Girls Grammar School in pleated gym frocks and squashed panama hats. We do Latin, French, English, bio, history, art and drama. Our father plays 'Mack the Knife' over and over again. He brings people home for dinner but he does not pay the bills. Our mother hides behind a door smoking a cigarette and crying. She uses Ponds Skin Cream. In her dressing table drawer there are chunky bracelets, white lace hankies and a red lipstick that she never uses. We are sisters. Judy buys a motor scooter. Vanya goes to art school. Robin falls in love. Brigid climbs the plum tree and falls down into the compost heap. In the wild garden we plant freesias, violets and snowdrops, but in the house the anger bruises our soft skin. On a cold, still day we go to our father's funeral. Forgive me, he asks, but that is easier said than done. We head off into our lives and have lovers, babies, breakdowns. Our mother says I hope you know what you are doing. She drives around in her little blue car helping the less fortunate. She is always there for us but then she dies. We are the four daughters of Irene Ethel and Robert William. At the funeral we carry our mother's coffin. A man says, can I help you but we say no, we know what we are doing. We blunder red-eyed back to our lives. We buy things at jumble sales. We make apple crumble and Irish stew. Our mother has taught us to make a little go a long way. Three of us have chunky legs but Judy has a decent pair. We marry a variety of men but it never quite works out. We give birth to five daughters and six sons between us and we give each one a middle name. We feed them carrot sticks and brown bread and squeeze grapefruit to make juice. We read them stories and we hold them tight. We agonise about our weight. We say to each other, do you think I should wear this? We say, that haircut really suits you, it makes you look younger. We say, you can have this if it fits you. Something is dreadfully wrong. Robin has gone from slightly odd to very ill. The doctors say she has a tumour wrapped around her spine. We do not know what to do. We visit her with bunches of roses, with books, with packets of biscuits and pasted-on smiles, but she dies. Goodbye, Robin Pansy Primrose Violet. We drink wine. We smoke a joint. We learn to meditate. We see a therapist. We know that every loss triggers the old losses. *Sometimes we live in the city, sometimes we live in the town, sometimes we take a great notion, to jump into the river and drown.* We are sisters. We paint. We write. We sew. We wrap things in brown paper. We hesitate at the lip of the sherry bottle. We love to swim. We love to dance. We love rivers, music, flowers. We give each other books for Christmas. We are growing old. We like to sit together on Sunday afternoons eating bran muffins and drinking tea and saying to each other do you remember when?

Happy Christmas Tessa

They were good times, weren't they, our summers at the river? They had a shape, a pattern which we held together and which held us. There were rituals which had to be observed. Everyone arrived on Christmas Eve, all the bits of our sprawling family, lovers and husbands and assorted kids in tow. Horns tooted and dogs barked and life tumbled about. The cars were bulging with great heaps of stuff: bedding, food, wine, books, instruments, new glittery ornaments to hang on whichever pine tree we decided was to be the one. We always used the same old golden angel though. Christmas Eve was singing and dancing, and if you were a child you joined in for as long as you could until you fell asleep and got tucked up in a bunk, draped in cobwebs and strange dreams. Then the adults would open another bottle and begin the filling of the stockings with delightful treasures. There had to be an orange in each stocking toe, and dried apricots and walnuts in shells, Japanese paper flowers that blossomed in water, mouth organs and whistling things, a paint box, chocolate coins, Puffin books and wind-up tin toys, the crazier the better. Someone would pull a joint from their pocket and the night would vibrate with music, laughter, fascinating worlds of extravagant truths and elegant possibilities. By the time the last person had a bedtime piss in the grass, the entire universe would have been deciphered and the sky would be lightening. Remember, the old radio playing jazz and the yellowed moon lolling in the languid trees?

Horribly early the children wake and rummage and exclaim and are sent back to bed until a more respectable hour. Then there is coffee, real coffee and croissants and peaches, and off we go. All of us together, making the expedition to the river. Slowly down the dry, pebbled road, past the cows, through the cool, ferny bush to the water. We lie on the bank. We swim. We float. We drift on striped rubber air beds. We row between mangroves, cutting the glassy water with the oars. Then en masse and dripping we walk back and proceed with Christmas Day, a symphony with endless minor variations. The children and a drunken aunty decorate the tree with tinsel and rainbows. Crepe paper ribbons scatter in the wind, glass balls shimmer. The angel with a star on her wand waves from the tip of the swaying pine. We have forgotten Jesus. We are concerned with The Lunch, which will come together gradually and of its own messy accord. Vera boils the pudding, stirs the custard and whips an Everest of cream. Harriet sips endless sherry and haphazardly dissects three chickens. Kiya and Jim bicker while producing elaborate salads. Ruby and Miles deal in the extraordinary: olive tapenade or mushroom roulade. One year it was a coulis of berries whirled in mascarpone, like blood in snow. They are sculptors, delighting in the manipulation of ingredients and shapes, the exploration of colour. Max is usually unhappy but has splurged on good French champagne.

Somehow everything comes together and we eat. Sitting on the deck in the afternoon, looking out at the smooth green river, drinking more than enough. Then we sprawl on rugs around the tree, because it is time for the Grand Ceremony, the giving and receiving of gifts. A middle child hands them out, one by one and slowly, while the ghosts of our parents and our grandparents laugh and whisper in the pine trees. Someone is falling in love and someone is falling to bits and someone else will soon leave the country. Nothing matters. We read books and eat and drink and talk and swim all summer long.

Those good days are gone. Summer is an arid affair in this distant city. The sun burns my eyes in a concrete supermarket car park as I buy resentful gifts for people who are almost strangers. On certain hot nights in separate lands, do your thoughts float like split mangrove pods up the Wade River as mine do? To escape the present we gild and dust our elegant memories, our faulty brilliant stories of the past.

Curriculum Vitae

Once I was a waitress at the Golden Dragon. Before that I worked in a bookshop that sold car manuals to men with greasy hands. Before that I was a hippie with a baby on my back and a diamond in my nose. Before that I was a school teacher who said sit down children once too often. Before that I worked in the tax office sorting papers into alphabetical order and wishing it was lunchtime. Before that I bought an old Citroën and backed it into a tree and sold it all in the same week. Before that I lived on an island with a one-armed trumpet player. Before that I ran a flea circus. Before that I lived in a household of musicians and caffeine was my drug of choice. Before that I got married and had twins and eggplants went mouldy in my fridge. Before that I wandered the streets of Cairo with a tattoo of a palm tree on my back. Before that I was a lonesome cowgirl and sat on a fence in a hat. Before that I lived in an attic in Sydney and could not be relied upon. Before that I did my PhD on postmodern architecture and the elegant shed. Before that I owned a small cafe that specialised in soup. Before that I cleaned motels in a seedy part of town. Before that I ran away from home on my bicycle with a satchel full of comics. Before that I was fat and happy in a white wicker pram. Before that I had a florist shop and sang to the roses. Before that I was a young girl in a photograph with mournful eyes. Before that I lived in Mexico and made sculpture out of glass. Before that I spoke seven languages and wrote love poems while sitting on a roof. Before that I played the fiddle for a bluegrass band and before that I was the best Scrabble player in the whole wide world.

Still Life: Journal Notes

Easter Monday. I buy fruit and vegetables at the market: coriander, lemons, tomatoes. The remnants of revelry on the streets of Subiaco. A ghost town feeling. A broken wine glass in a doorway and, for some strange reason, five Blue Castello cheeses squashed on the road. I hear singing in a foreign language coming from a doorway, joyous singing from an unseen woman who's cleaning an office building. Jesus would have approved. At home, I unpack my groceries, fry thick slices of tofu smeared with sweet chilli sauce and curry paste. Superb.

Wednesday. Grumpy. Various reasons. Bodily aches and pains. Can't remember – if I ever knew – how to do important grown-up things on my computer. Sad because we've stuffed the planet, and cancer is gnawing at various friends. Have realised that Leonard Cohen isn't going to invite me to the movies. Van Morrison is not going to ask me to dance. Maybe I need a partner. I will advertise. Ageing woman, reasonable body, interesting face, seeks man or woman for Scrabble, human touch, intelligent conversation and occasional languid sex. Should be able to acknowledge their own shadow and have a basic knowledge of Buddhism, Mexican cooking and Motown music. A shitload of money would be good, but I will consider you if you dress creatively and have an apartment in Tokyo.

Thursday. Here I am, late at night, in my house of teapots, trying to write a story which can never be fully told because it is about the dance of everything and I am not dead yet, so who knows where it will end? I've come to several conclusions lately. One is that it is easier to love people when they're not there. I can't remember the other one.

Friday. Days of gentle rain. We are not used to rain, here in this city on the edge of a desert, this place of endless summer. Birds on the lake. Feeling contented, after days of not.

Saturday. News of a death. My niece, aged fifty-six, of liver failure, caused by a lifetime of alcoholism. It is true, grief does make you numb. I set forth on my errands as if nothing is the matter and find myself weeping in a shopping center. I sit on a bench in the sun, remembering Rachel as a young girl, as an angry drunk, as a fabulous cook, as a kind-hearted mess, as someone who tried many times to get sober but did not succeed. As Josh Korda, one of my favourite Buddhist teachers, says: 'Drinking is a failed strategy for happiness.' Many people I know do not understand this.

Sunday. A warm autumn day. I am glad to be in my life, despite everything. I walk after dinner, watch the ducks gather by the lake, neat black shapes written in the dying light. I love the merciful blessing of dusk, the papery sound of birds rustling in the leaves. Under cover of darkness I steal a fragrant gardenia. I'd like to be the sort of person who buys herself fabulous flowers but I'm more the sort of person who cuts the mould off the cheese, then eats the good bit.

Monday. I go to my cooking job. I love shopping with someone else's money, leaving the kitchen spotless, the meals laid out elegantly. It's tiring though. I'm always glad to come home to raisin toast, pyjamas and telly. A hard day's work rewarded with a lazy evening.

Tuesday. Found poem, in *New Yorker* article about cosmetic surgery in Korea:

Reason you want surgery?

- Preparing for job
- Wedding
- Regaining confidence
- Suggestions from people

If you get the results you want from plastic surgery,
what's the thing you most want to do?

- Upload a selfie without using Photoshop
- Get a lover
- Enter a competition for face beauty
- Which entertainer do you most want to resemble?

For the record, I don't wish to enter a competition for face beauty. I don't want to resemble any entertainer and if people make suggestions I will tell them to go jump.

Anzac Day. A man in our apartment block died. His body wasn't found for several days. Last year I gave him a Christmas card and in return he came to my door with a little fruit pudding for me, so drunk I had to walk him back to his apartment. Another tragic death. Too much sadness.

I can't watch Anzac footage. There is no glory in war. If the dead could speak, there would be no war, as Heinrich Boll wrote. I've come down with a cold and wander around wrapped in my dressing-gown and self-pity, doing nothing much. This too will pass.

Sunday. Slow to wake after riotous circus of dreams, due to codeine taken for cold. Surface gradually, feeling groggy. Write letters. Walk slowly to my vegetable allotment, pick rocket, spinach, bok choy. An old boyfriend contacts me on Facebook. What a heartbreaker he was, that tall skinny boy with long straight hair and guitar-playing fingers. Now he's a bald psychiatrist who lives in Wales with his wife and their dogs. I adored him more than he adored me, all those years ago. Here we are, still friends somehow, due to the wonders of the internet. I cook my fresh-picked greens with carrot, ginger and garlic. A day of much-needed gentle.

Monday. Tuesday. Wednesday. Thursday. Forgot to write anything.

Friday. A day of errands. In the evening I go to my dharma discussion group, taking a proper cake featuring dates and walnuts and coconut topping. This month's topic is unsatisfactoriness. Seven of the ten members are psychologists, who work each day with human suffering. We talk about the second arrow. The first arrow is the unavoidable, the second arrow is the misery we add when we put ourselves at odds with what is happening. I walk home in the moonlight, happy to have spent time with kindred spirits who loved my cake.

Saturday. Go to an eco fair. Buy beeswax lip balm and honey from the Montessori School stall. Wish I'd done interesting things like looking after bees when I was at school. Then to Fremantle, where I bump into six different people I know. A city is also a village, it seems. Eat disappointing Indian food at the food hall and forget to buy a small quiet clock for the kitchen, but enjoy my day anyway. Intended to go walking with a friend tomorrow but he says the weather report is 'iffy with patchy uncertainty', so we'll sit on his sofa and talk philosophy instead.

Thursday. Once again there are lost days. Well, unwritten ones, anyway. But today is a cracker. The rattle in my engine is fixed and I don't have to find $3000 for a new transmission. Buy a soft lilac dressing-gown to celebrate. My granddaughter is learning to walk. Like a tiny sumo wrestler in her big warm jacket, she scrunches up her face and brings herself to standing using every ounce of her being. She steadies herself, takes a small step, then plops down onto the grass. I never saw a more beautiful thing.

Thursday, another one. The days drift by, warm autumn days, days of everything and nothing. Yesterday I met a friend, in her seventies, whose husband died some years ago. She recently began living with a new man. 'He makes me laugh,' she tells me. 'We're off to Italy.' I entertain feelings of envy, then go home, admire a photograph of my granddaughter and make myself a spinach and feta pancake, remembering to enjoy my life just as it is.

Friday. I wonder if other people's dreams focus on things going wrong? My dreams are generally freaky: mobile phones ruined, bees swarming inside my hollow body, a nightly parade of difficulty and disaster. I'm always glad to wake up, with the thought, 'Thank God, that was only a dream.' It would be worse if my dreams were fabulous and my life dreadful. However today was horrible. I fell out with someone over a project we were planning, and my granddaughter has croup. It is her first childhood illness, scary for her, for her parents, and for me. I light a candle and send healing blessings, but am mired in a fear state larger than warranted. The only remedy is to go to bed with a wheat pack and a book.

Saturday. My granddaughter's on the mend. She came by with her parents, who were picking up some food. She takes half a dozen proud steps now and has added 'duck' and 'nut' to her vocabulary. Each week brings new accomplishments. What hard work it is being a child, all that learning going on, but what joy to see her delighted with her own expanding world. As Iris Murdoch noted, one of the secrets of a happy life is a series of continuous small treats, so here's to children, toast, a telephone conversation with a friend, a hot shower, warm slippers.

Monday. An ordinary sort of day that I mooch through with little sense of achievement. When evening comes I slump on the sofa watching a Japanese chef cutting turnips into chrysanthemums.

Tuesday. Some things I've never done: drunk a cup of coffee, drunk a beer, had a pedicure, been to Turkey or Hong Kong. I will probably never drink a coffee or a beer. I doubt I'll get to Turkey. My years are running out. I hope I get to Hong Kong though. Perhaps there I shall go berserk and have a pedicure.

Wednesday. I find a box of Hanimex slides abandoned on the footpath. On the original box, in faded spidery cursive, it says *Melbourne and Adelaide December 1975.* I see no sign of either city, just tiny worlds of scenery with an occasional person standing, stiffly posed, in front of a mountain or beside a lake. In my imagination I am a younger person with magenta hair and a dragon tattoo. I produce an artwork based on these slides, a profound statement about identity and place, which is exhibited in an edgy Brooklyn gallery. Instead I take them to an op shop and leave them on a shelf beside the dusty old cameras.

I love abandoned things, especially paper ephemera. A friend has sent me a 1953 examination paper from The New York Public Library for Promotion to Grade 3 / Assistant Branch Librarian. It is on flimsy, pale brown paper, and has five sections. My favourite one:

> When faced with responsibility for handling any one of the following situations, what should you do? Answers will be graded on the basis of judgment and knowledge of policies and procedures.
>
> 1. A piece of library statuary lands on a child's foot. He is apparently unharmed.
> 2. A third grade, out for a walk on a pleasant Spring day, drops in at the library for an unscheduled and unannounced visit.
> 3. A reader whom you are assisting is annoyed because you leave her to answer an involved question on the telephone.

4. A mother complains that her daughter reads too many girls' stories and asks you to keep her from borrowing any more of them.
5. Mrs Green asks for your help in selecting an encyclopedia for her fourth-grade son.

How pleasant it is to dwell in the dusty, faded elegance of the New York Public Library, 1953, which happens to be the year I was born. It is much easier, somehow, on this cold afternoon, than thinking about the ending of my marriage. Most of my sorrow has been attended to, but odd remnants of grief and shame remain.

Thursday. I send an email to a friend, suggesting he have a good wee, when I meant a good week. *Festina lente*, hurry slowly, as my mother used to say, and always re-read your emails before sending them.

Friday. Two small disasters: a horribly burnt pot, and soy candle wax spilled all over my carpet. If this is my share of the suffering of the world so be it. In the grand scale of things, these are minor vexations.

Saturday. A friend does something that bothers me. Once I'd have written a long email, trying to fix it, unable to be with my discomfort. Now I leave it alone, merely observing my hurt and my anxiety. Allowing uncomfortable feelings is new for me but as the Dalai Lama replied when asked about his practice, 'After thirty years I think I can see a little improvement.'

Sunday. The grace of an ordinary day. Clean, dry laundry. An afternoon walk, admiring gardens. Vegetable soup on the stove, something decent to watch on the telly.

My life is charmed, even though I'm getting older and still don't like my hair very much.

Monday. The human mind is a mysterious thing. While making breakfast, the word 'ectoplasm' arrives, unrelated to anything in my dreams or anything logical. Ectoplasm, I say to myself, ectoplasm. It's a beautiful word. Later, in the supermarket, I notice a young Asian woman wearing a t-shirt with 'I am Not Sorry' written on it. I wonder if she understands how it relates to Indigenous issues in Australia, or whether it has some other context for her. I wish I knew if she was Japanese, Korean or Chinese.

Tuesday. The deadline for my book nears. A musician friend calls dead lines 'dead lions.' It is cheering to see the end in sight, although I am tired and can't find either of my pairs of glasses. There's an overabundance of rocket and bok choy in my garden. I give it away to anyone who'll accept. My neighbour reciprocates with oaty raisin biscuits. I didn't think I liked biscuits, but hers are good. Later the same day I find my glasses, one pair in a box of letters, the other perched on a shelf near the door.

Wednesday. I read a David Sedaris piece about huge spiders. Spiders are of little interest to me, per se, but his dry sense of humour and elegant way with words make it compelling. He describes a fly caught in a web as 'an angry raisin.'

Thursday. Happiness, when my son showed his daughter a worm from his worm farm. Firstly, because I have raised a fine son who has a garden and a worm farm. Secondly, because of the way my granddaughter responds. She looks at it carefully with a mixture of wonder and dismay, then turns and toddles away. I can almost hear her thoughts: 'No thanks, Dad. I don't want to touch it. I don't think I can eat it. In fact, I just don't like the look of it.'

Friday. I abandon my To Do list and go to the food hall instead, where I sit in the sun eating Thai takeaway and reading the paper. On the way home I drop a fifty cent coin into the sliding mechanism beside the passenger seat in my car. Most people would not have tried to retrieve it but I did. It's still down there but I dislodged a two dollar coin and a twenty cent coin, so now I'm a dollar seventy ahead. The other thing that happened today that might have been worth writing down has vanished so I give up and watch *Bright Star*, the film about John Keats and Fanny Brawne. It feels vaguely literary, thus not completely wicked, though no one would actually know or care whether I am working hard on my writing, or lying in bed snorting cocaine and dipping chocolate biscuits in whisky.

Saturday. Nearly bought some flash toothpaste, on sale for half price. Read the list of ingredients, eighteen of them, including titanium. Did not buy. Dislodged the fifty cent coin with a long pair of scissors. Most satisfying.

Sunday. Long slow breakfast, tucked up in bed, reading old glossy magazines from the op shop. How I love the pretend world where Scandi hipsters eat reindeer fed on sedge, moss and thrift, and a British chap called Drew Buckleton Hornby grows begonias in his summerhouse. In New York, artists and musicians do marvellous things, and in Paris there's a wedding in a ballroom decorated with eight thousand soft pink roses and dahlias. Here, however, it is time to get up.

Sunday. My book is nearly complete. No doubt I shall miss it when it's done, and wander round strangely for a while. 'A book is finished when nothing rattles,' James Lee Burke said.

Just one or two small rattles and I'm there.

Things of elegant beauty

RARE THINGS

Things with FAR to go

Things that are hard to sa

AWKWARD AND POINTLESS THINGS

Prayers and incantations

acknowlegments & reading list

Acknowledgements & Reading List

I am indebted to Sei Shōnagon for the lists of lists that punctuate the pages of this book. I hope these may inspire you to create some lists of your own.

I acknowledge the following titles, which I have drawn upon while writing this book, and which you may find useful:

Diane Ackerman. *A Natural History of the Senses.* New York: Vintage Books, 1990.

Jerome Bruner. *Making Stories: Law, Literature, Life.* Harvard, USA, 2003.

Helen Garner. *The Feel of Steel.* Sydney: Picador, 2001.

Natalie Goldberg. *Wild Mind: Living the Writer's Life.* Boston: Shambala, 1990.

Natalie Goldberg. *Long Quiet Highway: Waking up in America.* New York: Bantam Books, 1993.

Beth Kephart. *Handling the Truth: On the Writing of Memoir.* New York: Gotham, 2013.

Anne Lamott. *Bird by Bird.* New York: Pantheon Books, 1994.

Anne Lamott. *Plan B: Further Thoughts on Faith.* New York: Riverhead Books, 2005.

Pablo Neruda. *Selected Odes of Pablo Neruda.* Berkeley: University of California Press, 1990.

Mary Oliver. *Dream Work*. New York: Atlantic Monthly Press, 1986.

Gary Synder with Julia Martin. *Nobody Home: Writing, Buddhism, and Living in Places*. San Antonio: Trinity University Press, 2014.

Abigail Thomas. *Three Dog Life*. San Diego: Harcourt, 2007.

Abigail Thomas. *Thinking About Memoir*. New York: Sterling, 2008.

Audrey Yoshiko. *Enso: Zen Circles of Enlightenment*. Boston: Shambala, 2007.

Words from Michael Leunig's poem 'The Deficit' on p. 71 appear courtesy of Michael Leunig.

The following pieces were first published elsewhere: 'Jive' and 'The Zen Cook' in *Mind Moon Circle,* Journal of the Sydney Zen Centre, Winter 1996; 'Apricot' in *Southern Review*, Vol. 27, No. 3, September 1994; 'In The World' in *What Book: Buddha Poems from Beat to Hip Hop*, ed. Gary Gach, Parallax Press: Berkeley, 1998; 'Certain Difficulties' and 'Being a Poet' in T*omorrow All Will Be Beautiful,* Allen & Unwin: Sydney, 2007; 'Writing in America' in *The New Zealand Listener*, January 27, 2007; 'The Mirrored Surface' in *Naked Eye Magazine*, Curtin University, 1990; 'Good Voodoo – a Short Story' in Review of Australian Fiction, Vol. 16, Issue 4, 2015; 'Sisters' in *Westerly Magazine*, Vol. 42, No. 3, Spring 1997 as well as *Turbine* online journal, IML Victoria University, 2005; 'Happy Christmas Tessa' in *Summer Shorts Anthology*, Fremantle Arts Centre Press, 1993; 'Curriculum Vitae' in *Transitions Anthology*, ed. Justina Williams, City of Fremantle, 1996.

With thanks to my friends, my family, and my writing group, for believing in me and my work. Extra special gratitude to Sam Bodhi Field, Melissa O'Shea and David Nourish, for editorial suggestions. It takes a village to write a book and I am grateful.

CLOUDS

Winds

Flowering trees

BIRDS

Insects

Stars Games

TREES THAT HAVE NO FLOWER

First published 2016 by
FREMANTLE PRESS
25 Quarry Street, Fremantle 6160
(PO Box 158, North Fremantle 6159)
Western Australia
www.fremantlepress.com.au

Also available as an ebook.

Consultant editor Georgia Richter
Cover design Tracey Gibbs
Cover photograph from 'Kate's Teapot' by Jo Darvall © 2015, Watercolour on Reves paper, 16.8 cm x 19.5 cm. (Inspired by the creative life of impressionist painter Kathleen O'Connor 1876–1968.)
Printed by Everbest Printing Company, China

National Library of Australia
Cataloguing-in-Publication entry

Still life with teapot : on zen, writing and creativity
Brigid Lowry
ISBN: 9781925163544 (paperback)
Creative writing — Authorship.
808.02

Fremantle Press is supported by the State Government through the Department of Culture and the Arts.

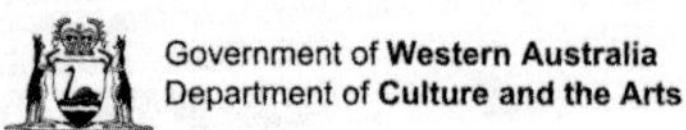

Publication of this title was assisted by the Commonwealth Government through the Australia Council, its arts funding and advisory body.